Piano Solo

THE WORLD'S GREAT CLASSICAL MUSIC

Great Piano Literature

67 Favorite Selections of Original Music for Piano

For Intermediate to Advanced Piano Solo

EDITED BY BLAKE NEELY AND RICHARD WALTERS

Cover Painting: Vermeer, *Open Window*, 1657

ISBN 0-7935-8255-5

HAL•LEONARD®
CORPORATION
7777 W. BLUEMOUND RD. P.O. BOX 13819 MILWAUKEE, WI 53213

CONTENTS

ABOUT THE COMPOSERS...

JOHANN SEBASTIAN BACH (1685-1750).

Johann Sebastian Bach's incomparable genius for musical form and structure is revered more than 300 years after his birth. Yet the Baroque master and his music were actually forgotten by the general public and musicians alike for many years. Musical fashions were already changing by Bach's later years, and his music was heard less frequently than in earlier in his lifetime. After his death, which may have been hastened by treatments and surgery for blindness, his music fell out of fashion. His second wife, Anna Magdelena, died in poverty about ten years later. Bach's works span a wide range of genres. He wrote liturgical works, Lutheran masses, church and secular cantatas, chamber music, organ works, orchestral pieces, concertos, vocal and choral pieces as well as compositions for clavier. In his day he was widely known as a virtuoso organist. His improvisational skills were legendary. With his contemporary George Frideric Handel, whom he never met, he was one of the last great composers of the Baroque era. Some ninety years after Bach's death, his works were once again brought before the public by the composer and conductor Felix Mendelssohn. Mendelssohn became a champion of the works of Bach and other composers who had been pushed aside with the shifting of musical fashions. Bach's music has been a mainstay of the international repertoire ever since.

LUDWIG VAN BEETHOVEN (1770-1827).

It is difficult to know how much of our perception of Beethoven is myth and how much is fact. He was the greatest composer of his era, certainly. Beethoven began his musical studies with his father, a Bonn court musician. He was appointed as deputy court organist in Bonn when he was eleven years old. He later continued his studies with Haydn, until differences between the two ended their relationship. Beethoven was first known to the public as a brilliant, flamboyant piano virtuoso, but there was a much darker aspect to his life. He was devastated when, in his late teens, he was summoned home from Vienna to keep vigil at his mother's deathbed. The second great tragedy of his life began when he was quite young, as a slight hearing impairment. In 1802, when the composer was 32, he was informed by doctors that he would eventually lose his hearing altogether. Beethoven sank into a deep despair, during which he wrote a will of sorts to his brothers. Whether or not he was considering suicide is a subject of some speculation. Whatever the case, the "Heiligenstadt Testament," as the will is known, states that he believed he would soon be dead. He eventually came to terms with his deafness and went on to write some of his most powerful pieces. His last six symphonies were written in the following years. In addition to his nine symphonies, Beethoven wrote pieces in nearly every imaginable genre. His works include an oratorio, two ballets, an opera, incidental music for various theatrical productions, military music, cantatas, a wealth of chamber music, some 85 songs and 170 folk-song arrangements. At Beethoven's funeral, on March 29, 1827, some 10,000 people joined in his funeral procession. One of the torch-bearers was composer Franz Schubert, who had idolized Beethoven. Some 45 years after his funeral, Beethoven's body was moved to the Vienna's Central Cemetery, where he lies near the grave of Schubert.

JOHANNES BRAHMS (1833-1897).

Johannes Brahms was a man of strong opinions. He disapproved of the "New German School" of composers, namely Liszt and Wagner. He avoided what he believed to be the excesses of the tone poem, relying instead on traditional symphonic forms. After his Symphony No. 1 was premiered, he was hailed as "Beethoven's true heir." The symphony, written when Brahms was forty-three years old, is so clearly linked to the symphonies of Beethoven that it is jokingly been called "Beethoven's Tenth." Brahms began his musical studies as a youngster, gaining experience in composition and working as an arranger for his father's light orchestra. He revered composer Robert Schumann. On the advice of Franz Liszt he met Schumann, with whom he developed a close friendship. He also developed a deep love for Schumann's wife Clara Wieck Schumann. From the time of Schumann's mental breakdown until his death in 1856, Brahms and Clara tended to the ailing composer. The truth of the relationship between Brahms and Clara Schumann remains something of a mystery. Brahms never married. Clara Schumann never re-married following Robert's death. When Clara Schumann died in May of 1896, Brahms did not get to the funeral due to a missed train connection. He died the following April. Throughout his life, Brahms would sign letters "Frei aber froh" (Free but happy), until his last years when he signed "Frei aber einsam," (Free but lonely). One of the pall-bearers at Brahms' funeral was the composer Antonín Dvorák.

FRYDERYK CHOPIN (1810-1849).

Although composer and pianist Fryderyk Chopin was born to a French father and spent half of his life in Paris, he alsways defined himself by the land of his birth, Poland. Throughout his life he retained strong nationalistic feelings. Chopin the pianist achieved the status of an idol. His mystique was based in part on his cultured upbringing, and in part on his fragile good looks. His sensitive nature, frail health, and self-imposed exile only intensified the public's fascination with him. In 1831, after receiving his training and achieved some success in Poland, Chopin moved to Paris. There he found himself one of many piano virtuosos. Although he quickely made a name for himself, his temperament and physical frailty, caused by tuberculosis that plagued him throughout much of his life, left him poorly suited to life as a performer. He gave only about 30 performances, many of which were private affairs. From 1838 to 1847 Chopin was romantically involved with novelist Georges Sand (Aurore Dudevant). The years of their stormy romance were his most productive as a composer. While Franz Lizst created works of grand proportions and brilliant virtuosity, Chopin remained a miniaturist, creating elegant, fluid melodies within the framework of small pieces. He was the only great composer who wrote almost exclusively for the piano. Chopin is set apart from other Romantic era composers by the fact that his works were not inspired by or based upon literature, works of art, or political ideals. Composition was difficult work for Chopin, who was a gifted improviser from his earliest days. He composed as he played, finding it painful to commit his work to paper. When Chopin and Georges Sand parted ways in 1847, the composer's frail health took a turn for the worse. He was further weakened by his 1848 concert tour of England. When he died in October of 1849, public fascination only increased, as evidenced by the nearly 3,000 mourners that attended his funeral.

CLAUDE DEBUSSY (1862-1918).

Claude Debussy saw rules as things to be tested. He repeatedly failed harmony exams during his student years, because of his refusal to accept that the rules were correct. Like many before him he took several tries to win the Priz de Rome. Debussy's musical language was affected by the music of Wagner, which he heard first-hand at the Bayreuth Festival, and Russian music. Another important event was exposure to the hazy harmonies of Javanese music. Yet the voice that he found was completely French. His music was as much a part of the Impressionist school of thought as the work of any painter. The composer also found his voice in periodic writings as a music critic. By breaking rules and composing in a style uniquely his own, Debussy led the way for a generation of French composers. His piano music was unlike anything the world had heard up until then, evoking a huge variety of sounds and harmonies from the keyboard. When Debussy died, after a long and painful battle with brain cancer, it seemed as though no one noticed. In fact, France was too consumed with war in 1918 to pause for the death of a composer, even the most important composer in the country.

ANTONÍN DVORÁK (1841-1904).

Antonín Dvorák's parents were firm believers that a child must learn to play an instrument and sing. Dvorák's father, an innkeeper by trade, was an avid amateur musician who played in the town band. But a career in music was unthinkable. The young Dvorák was expected to follow in his father's trade. After many battles the young musician was finally allowed to enter music school. After finishing his studies he took a job in an opera orchestra, taking on private students as well. By his mid-thirties he was supporting himself in great part with his compositions. Brahms, who later became his friend, helped him find a publisher for his work. His fame gradually spread throughout Europe and from there to the U.S. In 1885 Dvorák was invited to become director of the National Conservatory of Music in New York City. In his homeland, Dvorák had been both a fan and a student of folk music. In America he delightedly found a new style of folk music to study. He was particularly taken with the African-American spiritual. Yet he was homesick while in New York. Eventually he found a small Bohemian settlement in Spillville, Iowa, where he could spend his summers speaking his native tongue and generally relaxing in familiar cultural surroundings. In Spillville he worked on his Symphony No. 9, "From the New World". It was premiered in New York in 1893 and was a huge success. In 1895 homesickness took Dvorák back to Prague, where he became director of the Prague Conservatory. He continued to compose, but the disatrous premiere of his opera Armida in March of 1904 hurt him deeply. Two months later he died suddenly while eating dinner.

GABRIEL FAURÉ (1845-1924).

Like Beethoven, Gabriel Fauré suffered a gradual loss of hearing that he endeavored to keep a secret from both friends and colleagues. While many remained unaware of his deafness until after his death, his closest friends guessed the situation and ignored the composer's increasingly obvious condition. Fauré was widely respected during his lifetime as an organist and teacher. He was the director of the Paris Conservatory for many years, teaching composition to an entire generation of French composers. Among his pupils were Maurice Ravel and Nadia Boulanger, who would become the most influential composition teacher of the twentieth century. As one might suppose, Fauré had little time left over to devote to his compositional endeavors once his teaching and performing obligations were fulfilled. Summer holidays were his most productive times. He also had little time for romance, entering a marriage of convenience in his early forties. Fauré sought a distinctive voice in his compositions. Although he eventually found a delicate, restrained and understated style, it was slow to be appreciated by the public. He is now regarded as the greatest composer of French song.

EDVARD GRIEG (1843-1907).

Edvard Grieg holds a unique position in music history as not just the most famous of Norwegian composers, but as one of the only Norwegian composers to have achieved an international reputation. Grieg drew upon traditional Norwegian folk songs for the inspiration and basis for many of his pieces. His incorporation of national folk music into classical forms inspired musicians throughout Europe to do the same with the traditional music of their own countries. Although Grieg's Piano Concerto in A Minor is his best known work, it is not typical of style. Most of his pieces are small in scale, giving him a reputation as a miniaturist. Grieg's first music lessons came from his mother. When Norwegian violinist Ole Bull heard the teen-aged Grieg play the piano, he arranged for him to enter the Leipzig Conservatory in Germany. Although the young musician was terribly homesick, living so far from home, he enjoyed the opportunity to hear performances by such luminaries as Clara Schumann and Richard Wagner. After his studies in Germany, and later in Denmark, Grieg returned to Norway. Finding himself in demand throughout Europe, Grieg spent much of his career traveling. The recipient of honorary degrees from Cambridge and Oxford, Grieg was also honored as one of his country's foremost composers.

SCOTT JOPLIN (1868-1917).

Joplin's father was freed from slavery only five years before his famous son. Although composer and pianist Scott Joplin would come to be know as the "King of Ragtime," it would be more than a half a century after his death before his genius would be recognized. Joplin was one of the principal innovators in ragtime, a highly syncopated music that began as a dance accompaniment at clubs in the St. Louis area. Ragtime came to popularity in the Midwest at about the same time jazz began in New Orleans. Joplin landed a job as a saloon pianist in St. Louis in 1885. Following his appearance at the Columbian Exposition in 1893, he settled in Sedalia, Missouri, and began composing. Although his "Maple Leaf Rag" was initially turned down by publishers because of its difficulty, it proved to be the piece that brought Joplin his first taste of musical notoriety. By 1908 Joplin was in New York City, turning his attention to composing larger works. He tried his hand at an opera, A Guest of Honor. His dream of writing opera consumed him, taking up much time and money. No one was particularly interested in producing an opera by an African-American at that time. He finally used his own funds to produce his opera Treemonisha at an inadequate hall in Harlem in 1915. The performance was a failure. Following the Treemonisha premiere, Joplin's mental health deteriorated steadily until he was committed to the Manhattan State Hospital. He died there, in poverty, in 1917. His music was largely forgotten by the 1970s when his complete works were published by the New York Public Library. A number of respected concert pianists began to program his works. The film The Sting employed much of his music, and spearheaded a popular Joplin revival. Treemonisha was resurrected in 1972, and eventually played on Broadway. Joplin, finally recognized as an innovator in American music, was awarded a posthumous Pulitzer Prize in 1976.

FRANZ LISZT (1811-1886).

Critics of the Hungarian composer/pianist Franz Liszt, the most famous pianist in history, accused him of composing music that was little more than a vehicle for self-promotion. He was the greatest pianist of his age, and judging from accounts of his playing and the music he composed for himself, he may have been the greatest pianist who has ever lived. His limitless piano technique set a standard for concert pianists that remains in effect to this day. Liszt was a larger-than-life character who generously supported the work of other composers and single-handedly invented the modern piano recital. His romantic life was legendary. He lived for many years with the Countess Marie D'Agoult, although she was married to another man. Liszt fathered two children with the Countess (one of whom would later marry conductor Hans von Bülow, only to leave him for composer Richard Wagner). Liszt later entered a romance with Princess Carolyne Sayn-Wittgenstein, for whom he left the concert stage and became Kapellmeister to the Grand Duke of Weimar. For a decade he lived in Weimar, writing and refining much of the music for which he is known. In his later years he took minor orders in the Roman Catholic church. Liszt was a generous teacher and taught a large number of students, exerting a profound influence over music-making in Europe for decades. He was also a conductor, and lead premieres of new works by Wagner, Berlioz and Verdi. As a composer Liszt looked to the future. His melodrama, "Der träurige Mönch," an atonal composition based on a tone row, clearly foreshadowed the subsequent work (decades later) of Arnold Schönberg. Public fascination with Liszt, the most famous celebrity in Europe, continued throughout his life. Not long before he died he celebrated his seventy-fifth birthday by embarking on a Julilee tour that received press coverage around the world.

FELIX MENDELSSOHN (1809-1847).

While most of Mendelssohn's colleagues could tell stories of their battles with family over choice of career and even more tales of their financial struggles as musicians, Felix Mendelssohn could only listen. He was born into a wealthy family that supported his goals in music from the very first. Even in their conversion from Judaism to Christianity, which the family had long considered, they were spurred to action by thoughts of their son's future. It was at the time of their conversion that they changed the family surname to Mendelssohn-Bartholdy. Mendelssohn set out on his musical career with two clear goals. He wanted to re-introduce the largely forgotten music of old masters such as Bach to the public, and he dreamed of opening a first-rate conservatory. At the age of twenty he conducted a pioneering performance of Bach's St. Matthew Passion, the first of many such concerts he would lead. A few years later he founded and directed the Leipzig Conservatory. As a composer, Mendelssohn combined the expressive ideals of the Romantics with the traditional forms of the Classical era. He is remembered both as one of the great Romantic composers and one of the last of classicists. In his career Mendelssohn found success at an early age, and remained highly successful until his death. His sister, to whom he was exceptionally close, died suddenly on May 14, 1847. Shortly after he got the news of his sister's death, Mendelssohn fell unconscious, having burst a blood vessel in his head. Although he recovered from this incident, he was terribly diminished by the illness. His health and mental state deteriorated until his death on November 4 that same year. Memorial services for the great conductor/composer were held in most German cities, as well as in various cities in Great Britain, where he had become quite a celebrity.

WOLFGANG AMADEUS MOZART (1756-1791).

It is exceptional for nature to produce such a prodigy as Mozart. Playing capably at age three, composing at five and concertizing throughout Europe at age six, Mozart was clearly remarkable, even for a prodigy. But for nature to have placed two prodigies in one household is beyond belief. Mozart's sister Marianne (Nannerl), a few years older than Mozart, was also a prodigy and was also featured on these concert tours. The young musician's parents moved heaven and earth to further offer Mozart every opportunity to perform on the clavier, organ and violin, and to make money. They traveled Europe from the time Mozart was 6 until he was about 17. As an adult, Mozart had difficulties in his relationships with his employers, and with colleagues. Pop culture has presented us with a caricature image of the composer, thanks in great part to the film Amadeus, in which he is painted as a freakish, spoiled child that refused to grow up. He was, in fact, impetuous and, likely as a result of his star status as a child, often difficult to deal with. But there was more depth of personality and musicianship than the film attempted to convey. Mozart was known to complete an entire symphony in a single carriage ride, yet he chafed at accusations that it was not work for him to compose. Another factor in the exaggerated stories of his character was his inability to handle financial matters. Although he was well paid for many of his compositions, he was in constant financial difficulty. He was frequently forced to borrow money from family and friends. Mozart, who more than any other composer represents the Classical era, tried his hand at virtually every musical genre available, and succeeded across the board. In 1791 Mozart received a commission to compose a requiem. According to the terms, the source of the commission was to remain anonymous. The piece proved to be the composer's own requiem, in that he died of a 'fever" before it was completed. The circumstance of his death, and the anonymous Requiem commission, gave rise to great speculation at the time, and a film some two centuries later.

SERGEI RACHMANINOFF (1873-1943).

Once described by composer Igor Stravinsky as "a six-and-a-half-foot-tall scowl," Sergei Rachmaninoff's stern visage was a trademark of sorts. Rachmaninoff first found fame as a pianist, touring throughout his native Russia to critical acclaim. His compositions won notice in those early years as well, including a Moscow Conservatory Gold Medal in composition. Yet the 1897 premiere of his Symphony No. 1 was a complete failure, due in large part to poor conducting by Alexander Glazunov. The dismal reception of the piece sent Rachmaninoff into a three-year creative slump that he overcame through hypnosis. During those three years he began conducting, earning international respect for his work on the podium. When his Symphony No. 1 received its London premiere in 1909, it was a huge success. Rachmaninoff made his first U.S. tour in 1909. On the tour he featured his Piano Concerto No. 3, which he had written expressly for his American audiences. Rachmaninoff fled Russia in the wake of the October Revolution of 1917. He brought his family to America where he continued to concertize, but did not compose for nearly a decade. After years of touring, Rachmaninoff decided that the 1942-43 concert season would have to be his last. In January of 1943 he began to suffer from an illness diagnosed as pleurisy. He gave what was to be his final performance on February 17. He then returned to his Beverly Hills home where he died of cancer on March 28.

FRANZ SCHUBERT (1797-1828).

The story of Schubert's life reads like a heartbreaking novel. Now hailed as one of the great Romantic composers, not one of Schubert's symphonies was performed during his lifetime. It was five decades after his death before any of them were published. Schubert, the son of a school headmaster, was not a virtuoso musician. Although his musical abilities were readily apparent to his teachers, his inability to perform left him with little means to support himself. He taught in his father's school for a time, but was miserable in that job. Schubert studied with Salieri, who was astounded by the young composer's abilities. After writing his first symphony at age fifteen, Schubert presented Salieri with a completed, fully orchestrated opera two years later. Schubert lived less than thirty-two years, yet he composed a phenomenal amount of music, including some six hundred songs. One hundred and forty-four of those songs date from the year 1815, a year in which he was teaching at his father's school. After Schubert left his father's school, he had the good fortune to collect a small group of devoted friends and supporters. The friends would periodically organize evenings of the composer's music, which came to be known as "Schubertiades." Schubert's health began to fail as early as 1822. When he died, at age thirty-one, he was viewed as a the composer of songs. It was not the enormous number of songs that earned him this mistaken designation so much as the fact that almost none of his other music had been performed during his lifetime. In addition to the songs, Schubert completed seven symphonies, and left one unfinished. He wrote a number of operas, although these are far from his best works. He also wrote choral works, chamber music and piano pieces. In accordance with his dying wish, he was buried beside Beethoven, whom he had idolized and at whose funeral he served as a torch-bearer.

ROBERT SCHUMANN (1810-1856).

Robert Schumann's dream was to become a pianist. As the son of a German bookseller and writer, he grew up surrounded by literature and instilled with a love of music. His world crumbled however, when he was just sixteen, with the death of his father and the subsequent suicide of his sister. Schumann entered law school, but spent most of his time studying music. In 1830 he moved into the household of his piano teacher, Friedrich Wieck. Soon afterwards, his left hand began to trouble him. His career dreams were shattered when his left hand became permanently crippled. He turned his energies to composition, making a name as a music critic as well. An inspired critic, he founded the music journal Neue Zeitschrift für Musik, in 1834. He often wrote under the pseudonyms "Florestan" and "Eusebius," Schumann fell in love with with his teacher's daughter, Clara Wieck, a highly acclaimed concert pianist. Clara's father fought vigorously against the romance. Schumann married Clara in 1840, but only after he had taken his case to the courts. In the year he was married, the composer wrote some 150 songs, turning to orchestral music the following year. Schumann suffered from bouts of terrible depression, which became progressively worse with time. In 1854 he attempted suicide. Unable to function any longer, he was then placed in an asylum, where he spent the last two years of his life. His wife and his friend, the young composer Johannes Brahms, looked after him in those final years.

PYOTR IL'IICH TCHAIKOVSKY (1840-1893).

It is a curious twist of fate that the composer of so bombastic a work as the 1812 Overture should have been an extremely fragile individual. Exceptionally sensitive from childhood, Tchaikovsky eventually deteriorated into a precarious emotional state. Tchaikovsky's musical abilities were already quite evident by age five, as was his hypersensitivity. His mother died when he was fourteen, a painful event that some say prompted him to compose. Over the years he was plagued by sexual scandals and episodes we might call "nervous breakdowns" today. Historians have uncovered evidence that his death, which was officially listed as having been caused by cholera, was actually a suicide. Many believe that the composer knowingly drank water tainted with cholera. Tchaikovsky's work stands as some of the most essentially Russian music in the classical repertoire, yet he was not a part of the Russian nationalistic school. In fact he was treated quite cruelly by critics of his day. "Tchaikovsky's Piano Concerto No. 1, like the first pancake, is a flop," wrote a St. Petersburg critic in 1875. A Boston critic claimed that his Symphony No. 6 ("Pathétique") "...threads all the foul ditches and sewers of human despair; it is as unclean as music can well be." For all the vehement criticism the composer received during his lifetime, his works are now among the best loved of the classical repertoire. His ballet The Nutcracker is an international holiday classic, while Swan Lake is staple in the repertoire of ballet companies throughout the world. His 1812 Overture is among the most recognizable of all classical pieces. In 1893 the composer completed work on his Symphony No. 6. The first movement dealt with themes of passion, the second with romance, the third with disillusionment and the finale with death. The piece was premiered on October 28. Nine days later the composer was dead.

Bourrée
from ENGLISH SUITE NO. 2

Johann Sebastian Bach
1685-1750

[Molto allegro]

[*mf*]

Fine

D.C. al Fine

Menuet
from PARTITA NO. 1

Johann Sebastian Bach
1685-1750

Prelude in C Major
from THE WELL-TEMPERED CLAVIER, BOOK 1

Johann Sebastian Bach
1685-1750

[rit.]

Two-Part Invention No. 8
in F Major

Johann Sebastian Bach
1685-1750

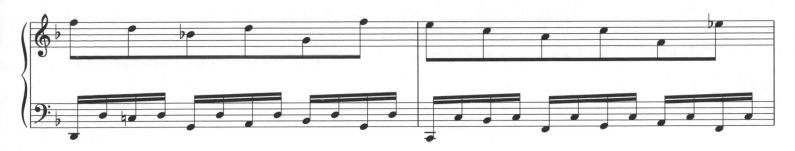

Two-Part Invention No. 1
in C Major

Johann Sebastian Bach
1685-1750

[Allegro]

[mf]

Bagatelle

Ludwig van Beethoven
1770-1827
Op. 126, No. 5

Allegretto

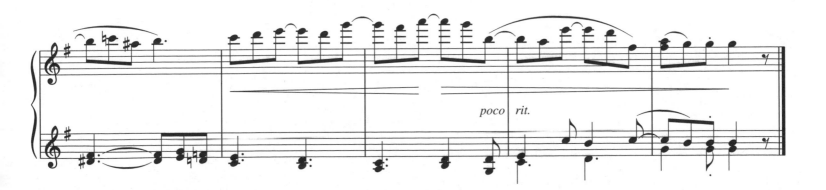

Turkish March
from THE RUINS OF ATHENS

Ludwig van Beethoven
1770-1827
Op. 113

Allegretto

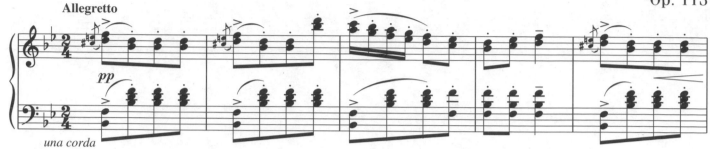

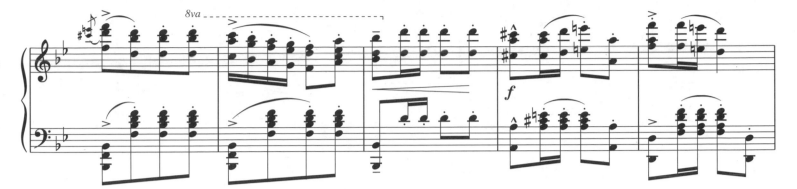

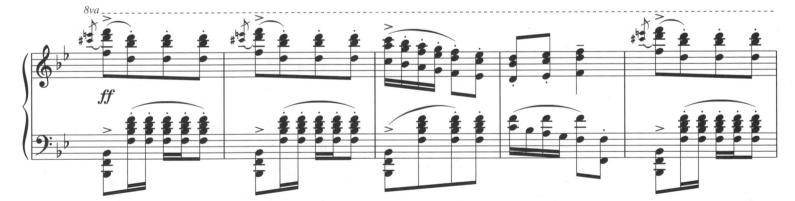

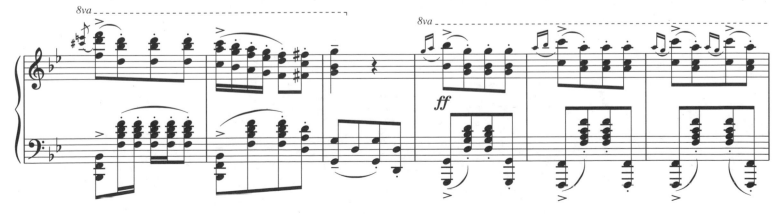

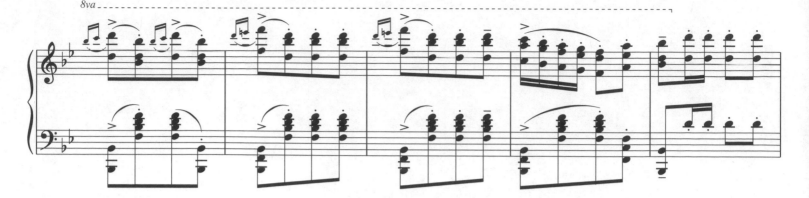

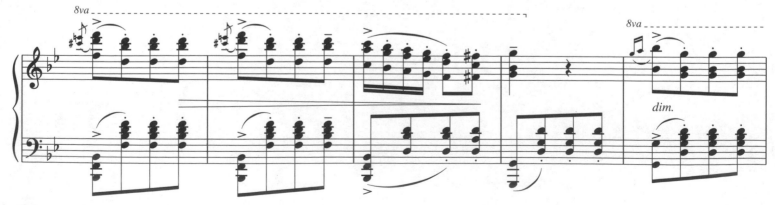

"Moonlight" Sonata
(Sonata in C-sharp Minor)
First Movement

Ludwig van Beethoven
1770-1827
Op. 27, No. 2

Adagio sostenuto

Si deve suonare tutto questo pezzo delicatissimamente e senza sordino.

sempre **pp** *e senza sordino*

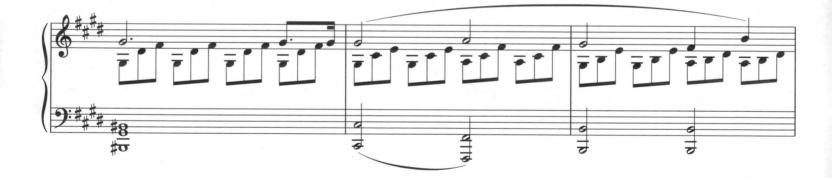

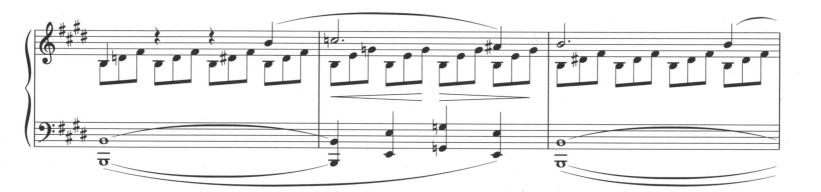

cresc.

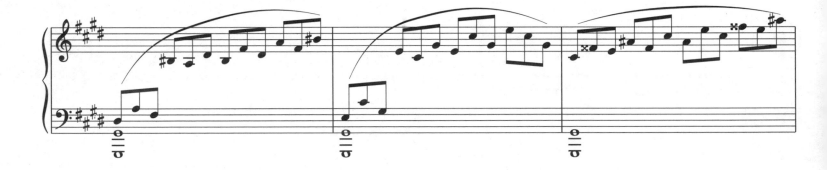

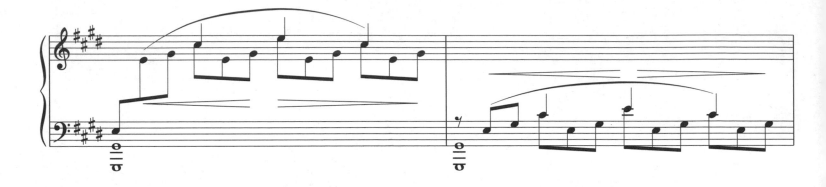

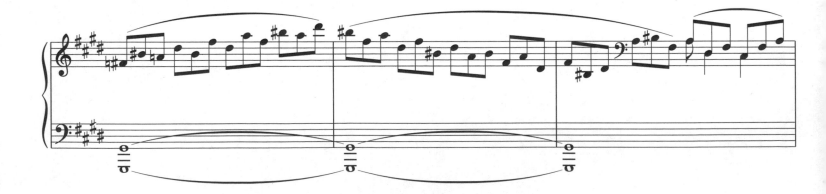

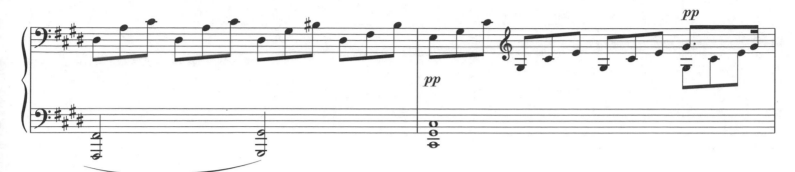

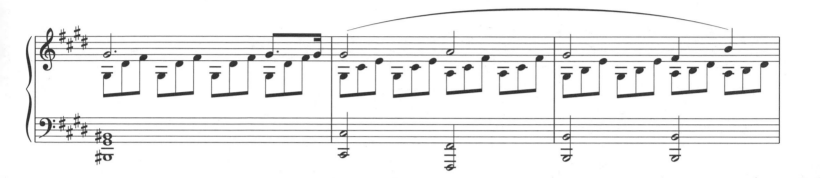

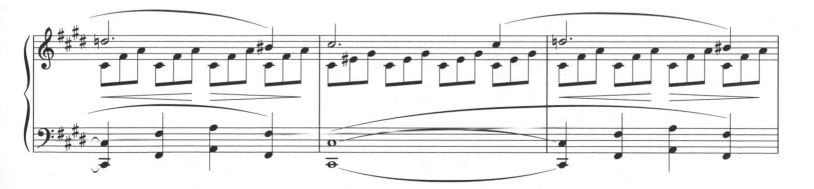

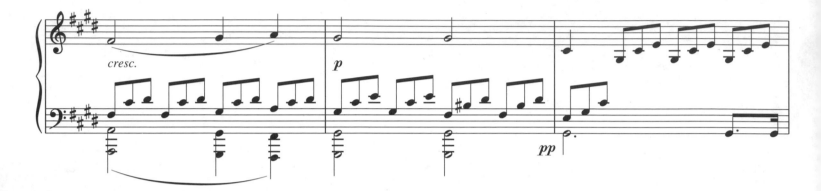

Intermezzo in F Minor

Johannes Brahms
1833-1897
Op. 118, No. 4

Allegretto un poco agitato

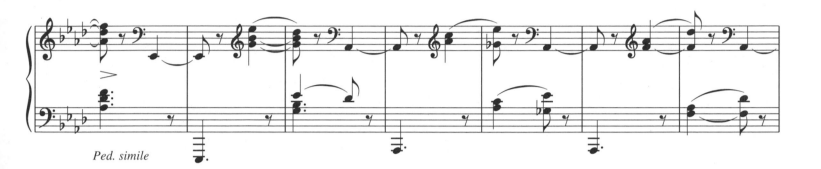

Waltz in A-flat Major

Johannes Brahms
1833-1897
Op. 39, No. 15

Intermezzo in B-flat Major

Johannes Brahms
1833-1897
Op. 76, No. 4

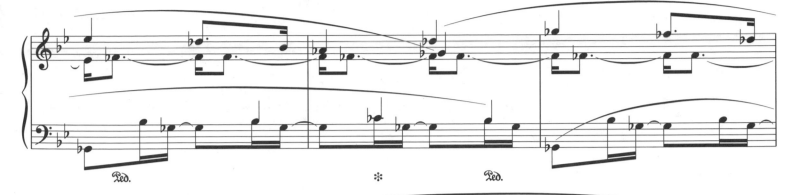

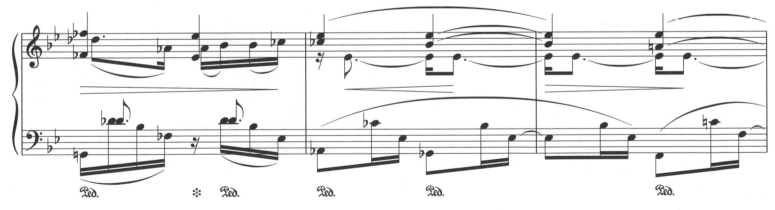

Mazurka in A Minor

Fryderyk Chopin
1810-1849
Op. 68, No. 2

49

poco a poco riten.

Ped. ✳

Tempo I

Ped. ✳ Ped. ✳ Ped. ✳ Ped. ✳ Ped. ✳ Ped. ✳

Ped. ✳ Ped. ✳ Ped. ✳ Ped. ✳

a tempo

rit.

Ped. ✳ Ped. ✳ Ped. ✳ Ped. ✳

Ped. ✳ Ped. ✳ Ped. ✳ Ped. ✳ Ped. ✳

Fantaisie-Impromptu
in C-sharp Minor

Fryderyk Chopin
1810-1849
Op. 66

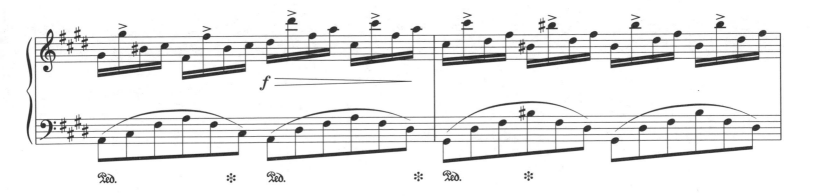

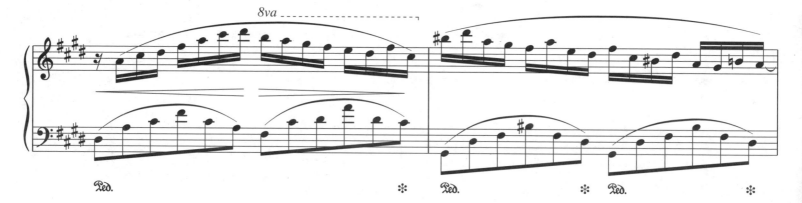

53

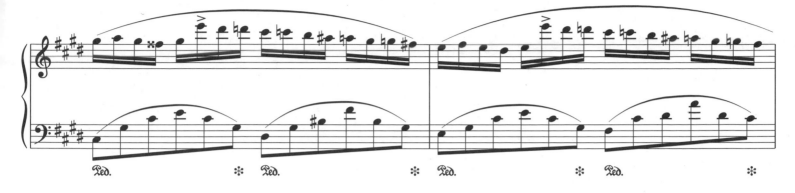

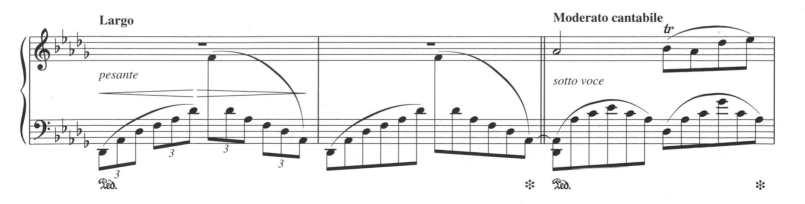

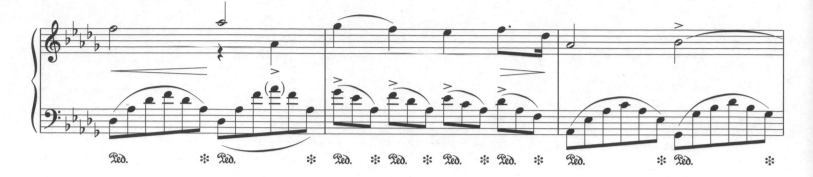

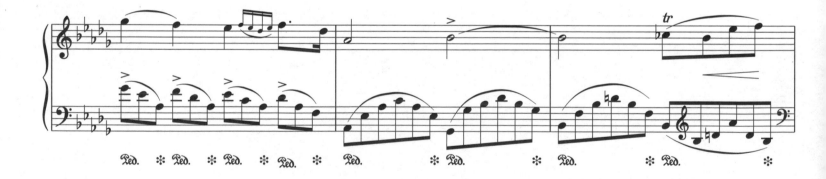

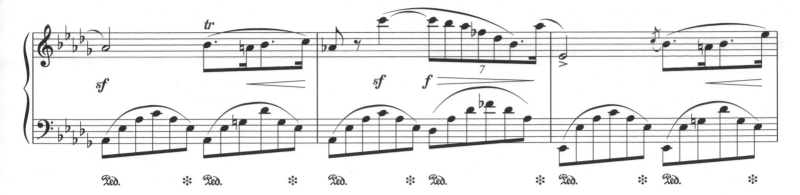

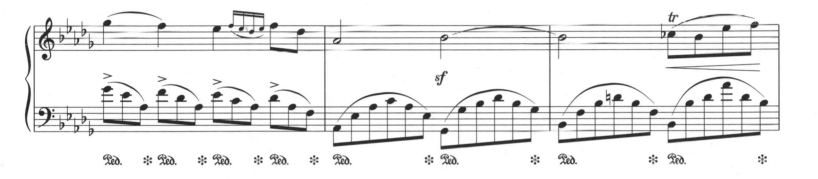

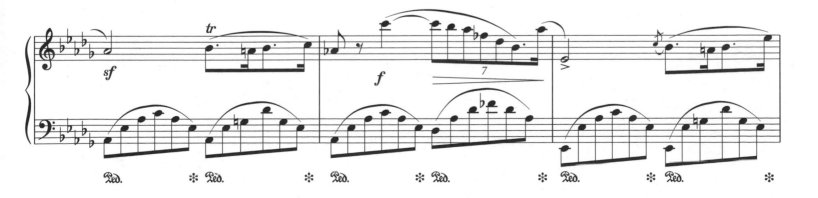

Tempo I (Allegro agitato)

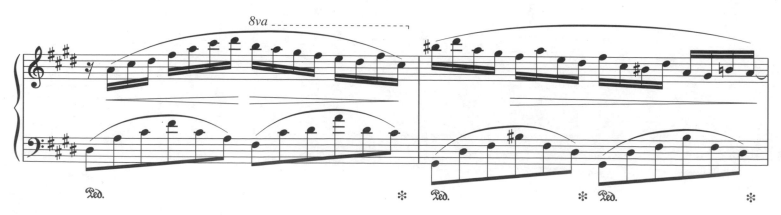

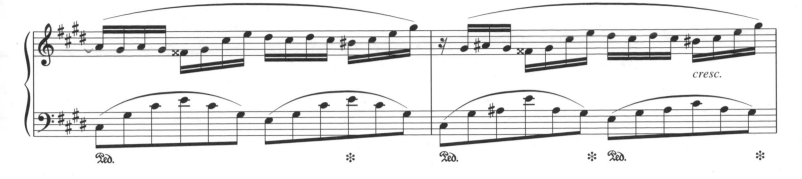

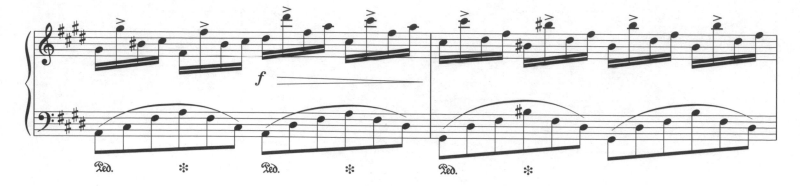

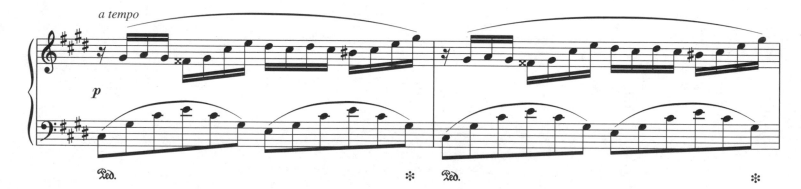

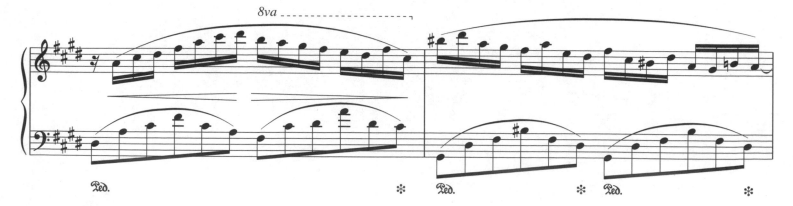

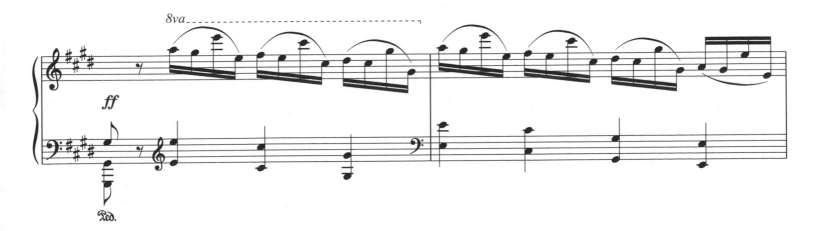

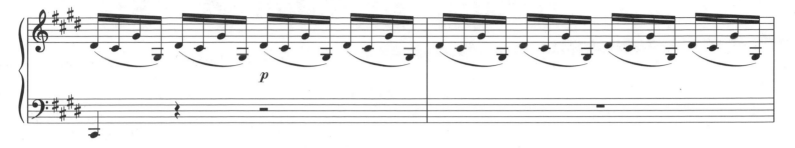

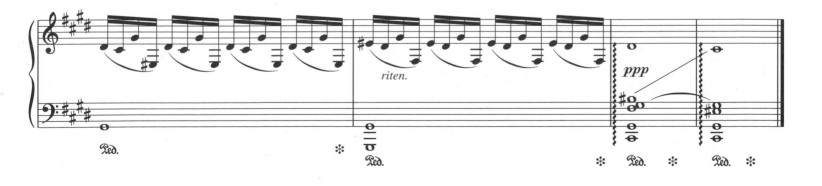

Nocturne in E Minor

Fryderyk Chopin
1810-1849
Op. 72, No. 1
(Posthumous)

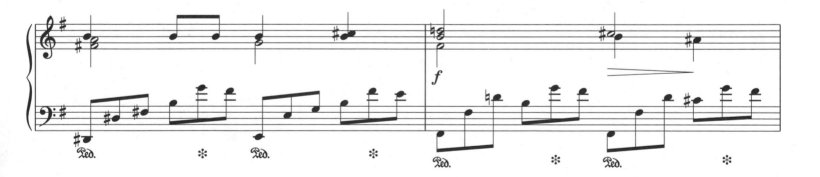

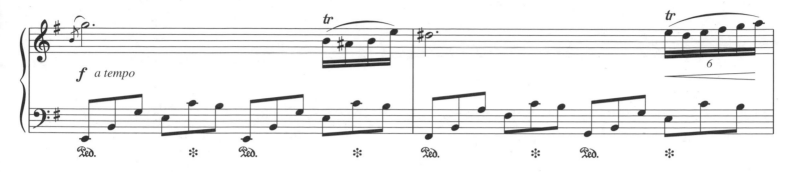

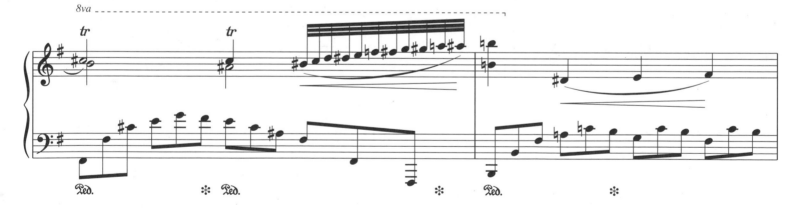

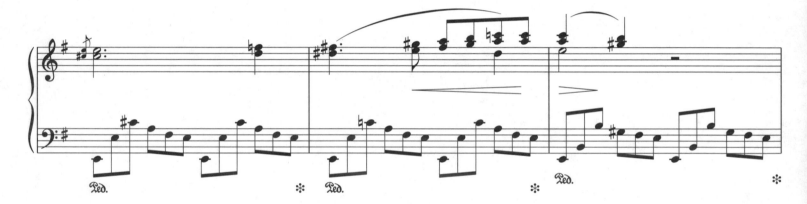

Waltz in D-flat Major
("Minute Waltz")

Fryderyk Chopin
1810-1849
Op. 64, No. 1

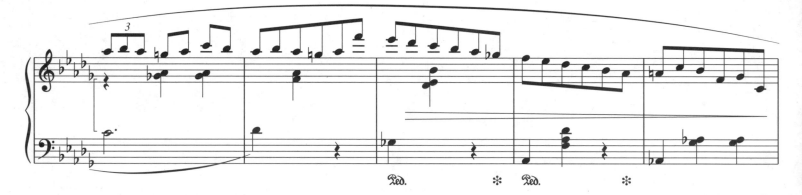

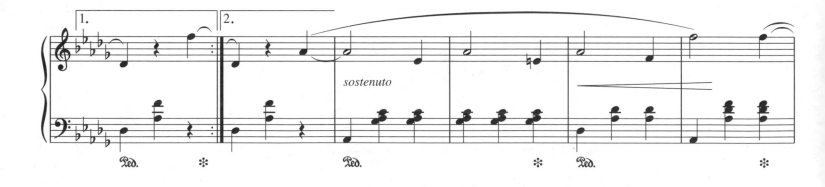

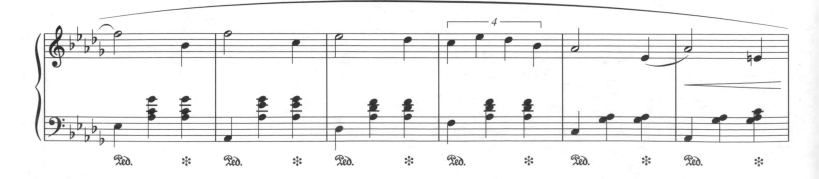

71

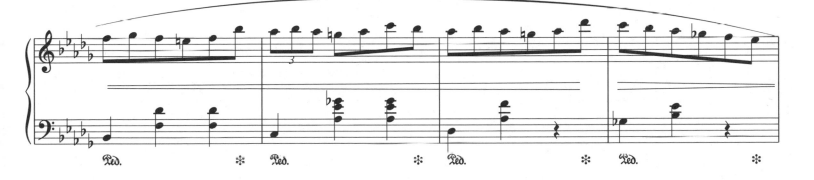

Waltz in A-flat Major

Fryderyk Chopin
1810-1849
Op. 69, No. 1

Lento (♩ = 138)

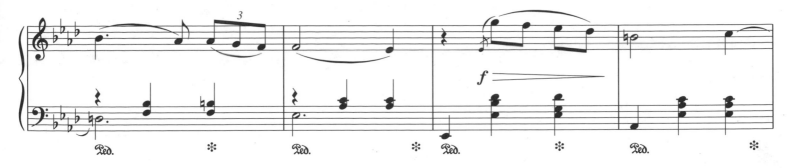

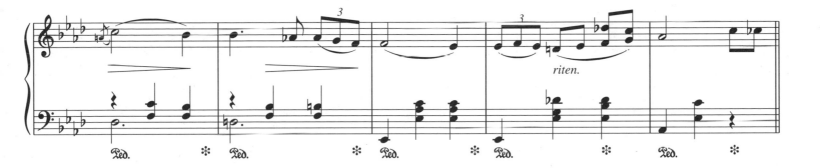

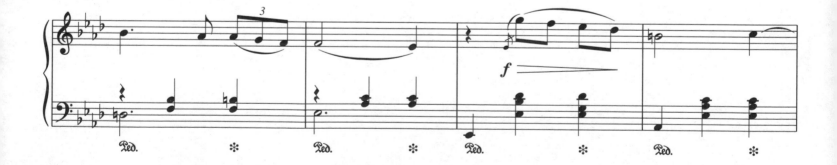

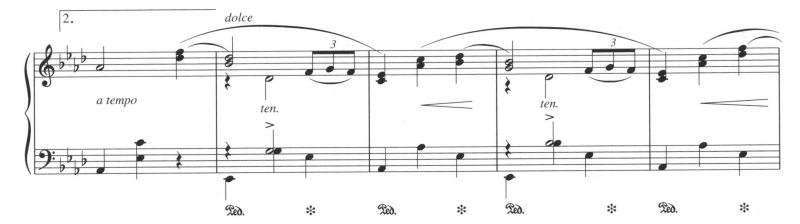

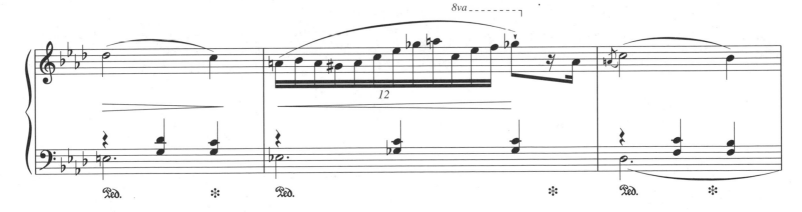

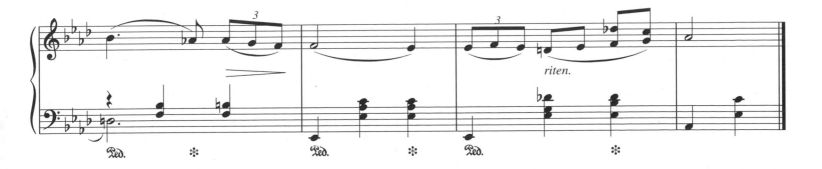

Prelude in D-flat Major
("Raindrop")

Fryderyk Chopin
1810-1849
Op. 28, No. 15

Sostenuto

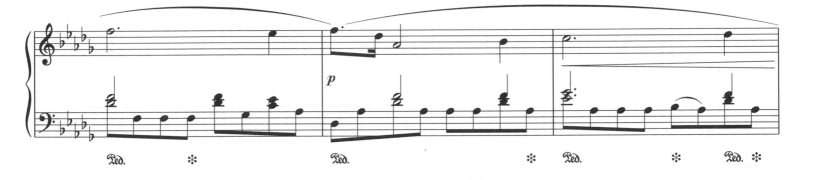

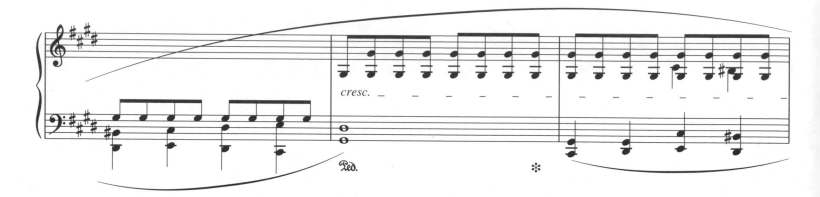

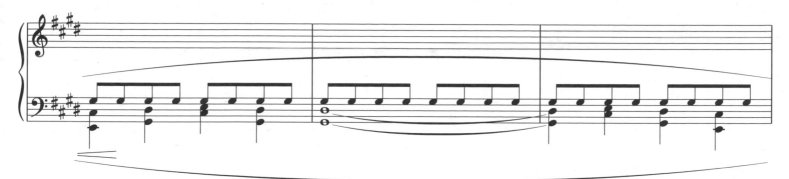

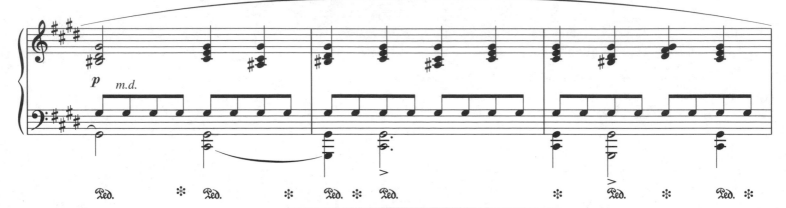

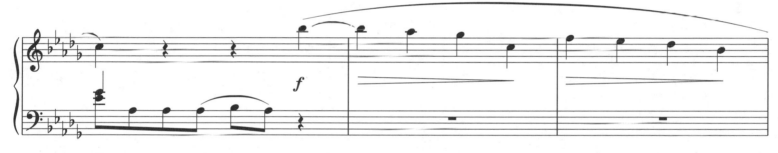

Rêverie

Claude Debussy
1862-1918

Andante sans lenteur (not too slowly)

pp *très doux et très expressif*
(gently, expressively)

meno p

mf

dim.

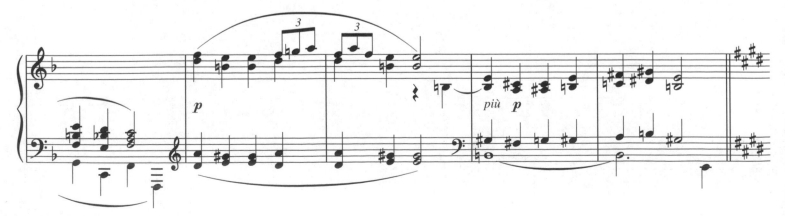

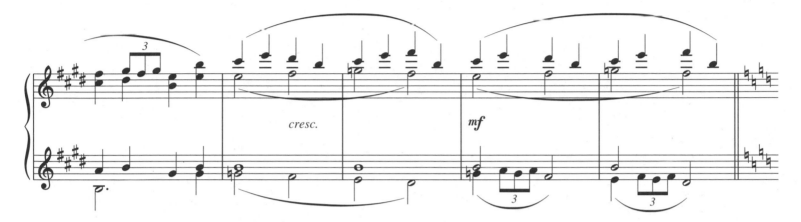

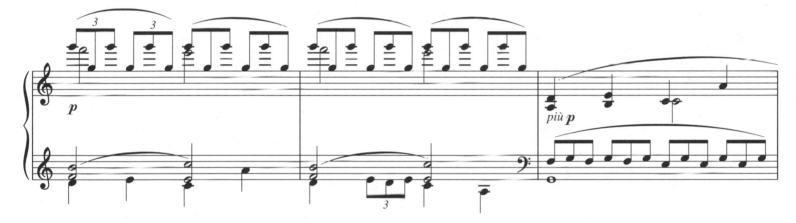

(l.h.)

meno **p**

p

p

un peu retenu
(a little slower)

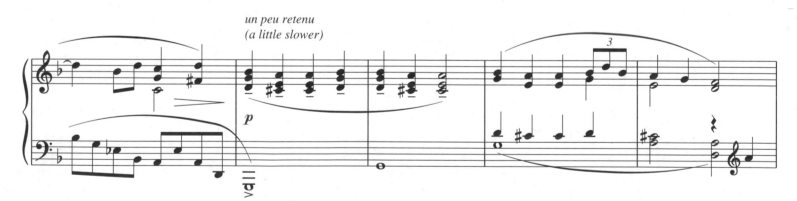

p

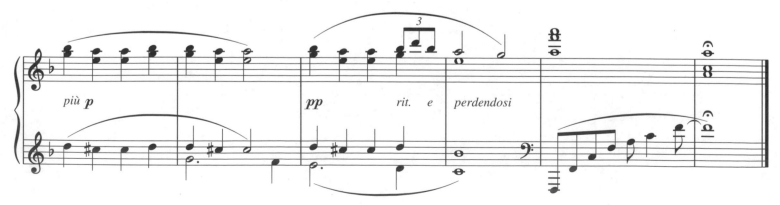

più **p**

pp

rit. e perdendosi

The Girl with the Flaxen Hair
(La fille aux cheveux de lin)

Claude Debussy
1862-1918

Très calme et doucement expressif (♩ = 66)

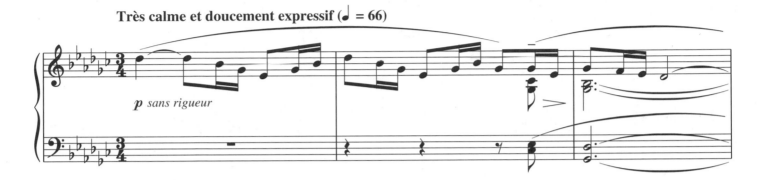

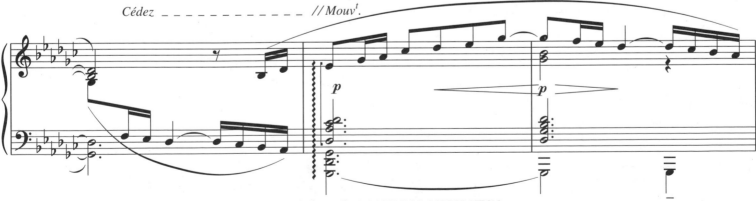

più p

(très peu)

p   *p*   *p*

un peu animé

p

mf

Cédez _ _ _ _ _ _ _ _ '' au Mouv ! (sans lourdeur)

pp

Golliwogg's Cake-walk

from CHILDREN'S CORNER

Claude Debussy
1862-1918

Allegro giusto

Poco meno mosso

94

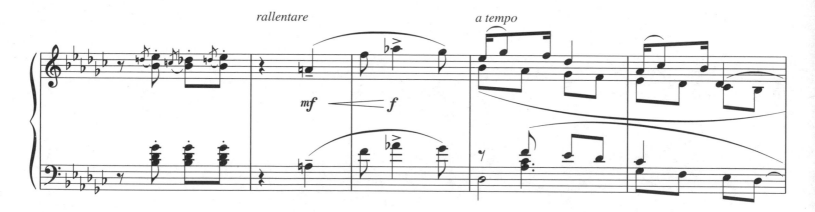

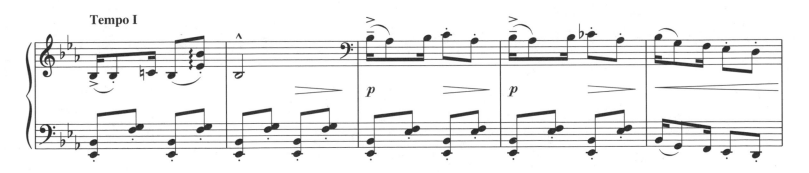

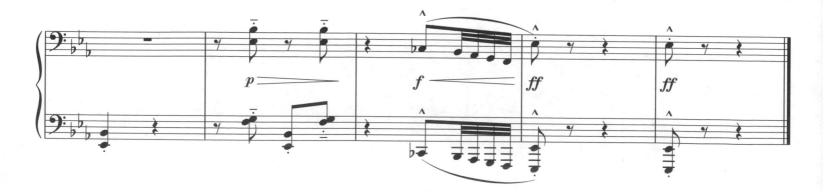

Doctor Gradus ad Parnassum
from CHILDREN'S CORNER

Claude Debussy
1862-1918

Animato ma non troppo

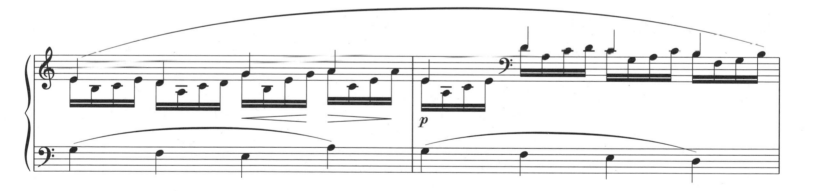

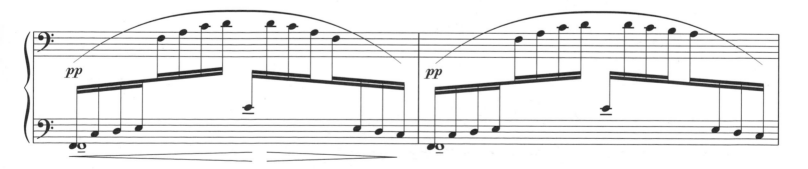

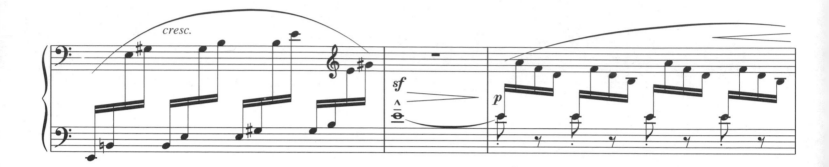

poco ritenuto

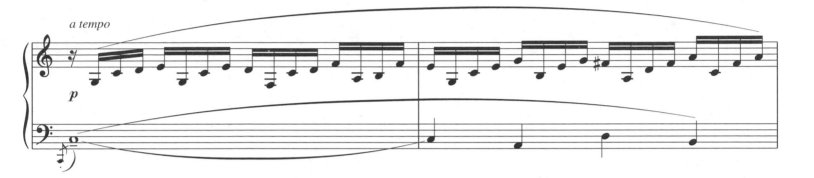

a tempo

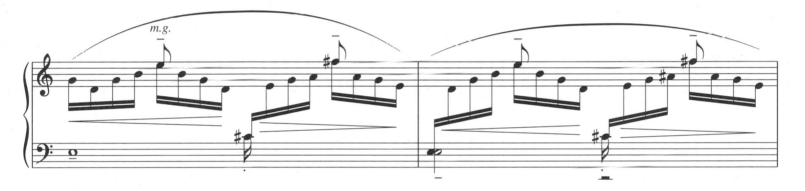

m.g.

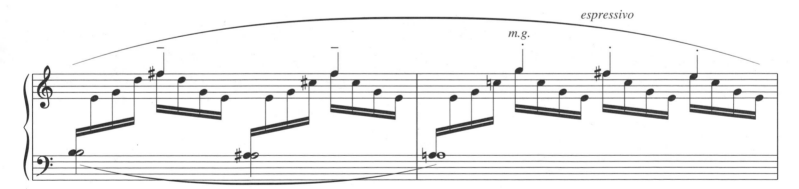

espressivo

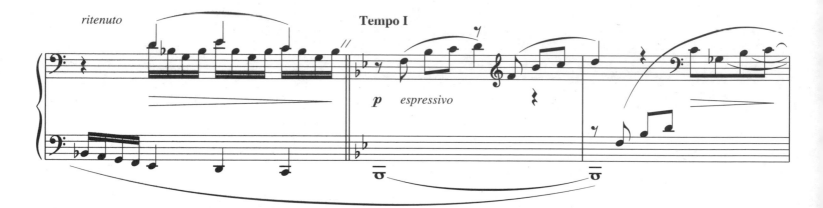

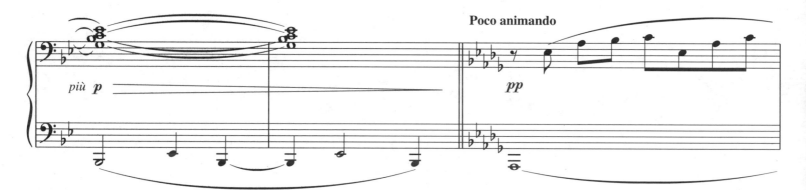

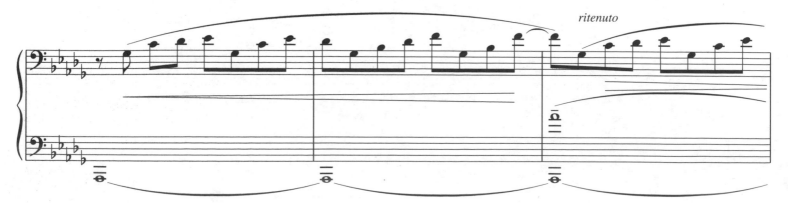

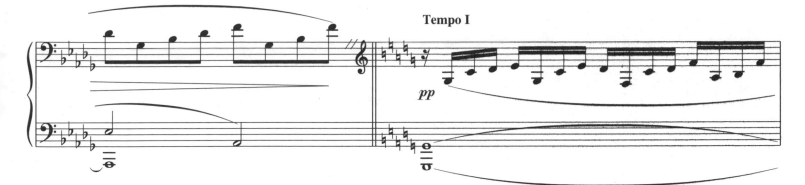

Tempo I

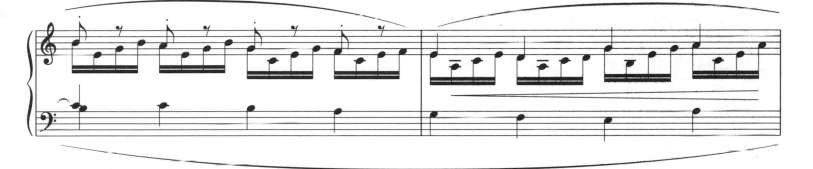

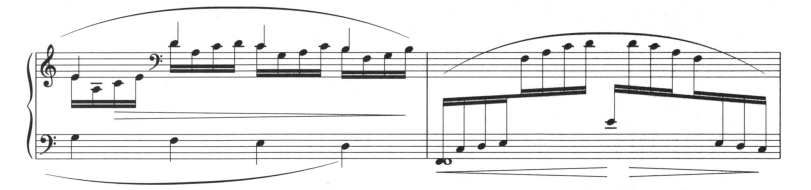

molto animato

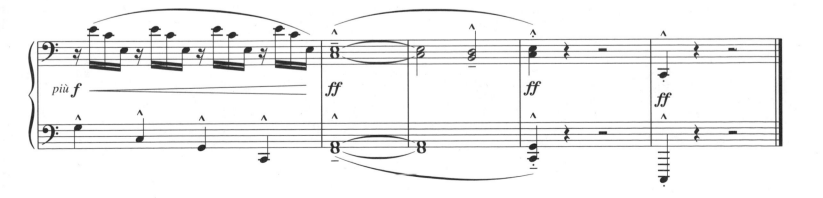

Le petit nègre

Claude Debussy
1862-1918

Allegro giusto

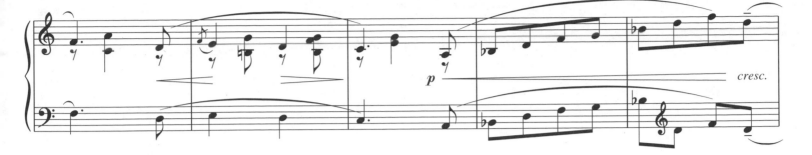

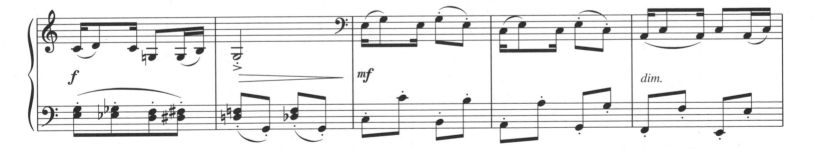

Humoresque

Antonín Dvořák
1841-1904
Op. 101, No. 7

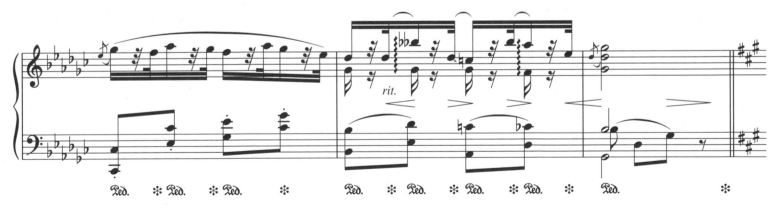

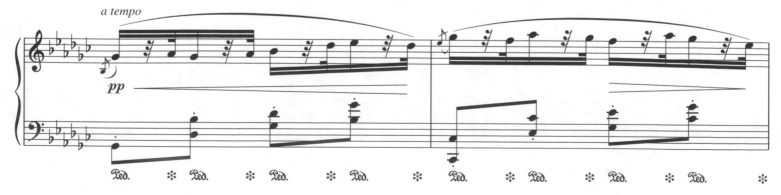

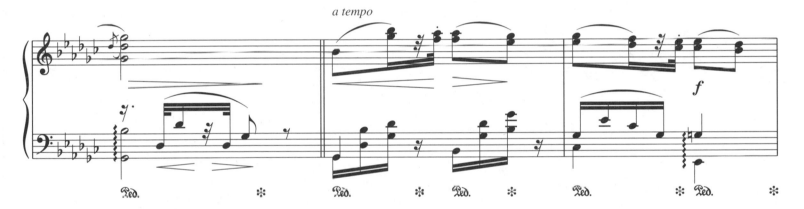

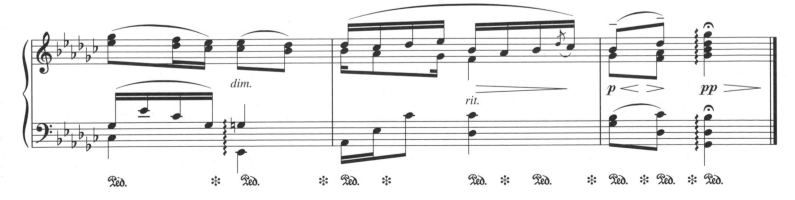

Romance sans paroles

Gabriel Fauré
1845-1924
Op. 17, No. 3

Andante moderato ♩ = 63

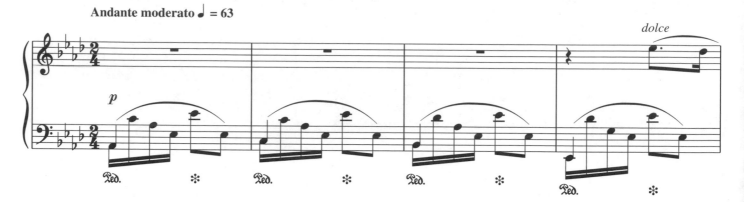

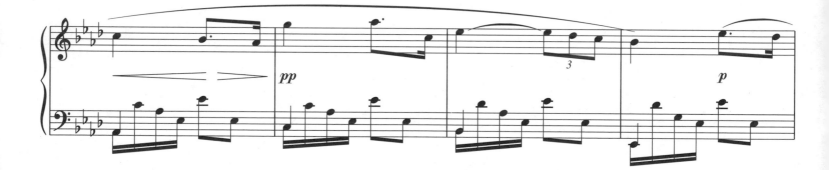

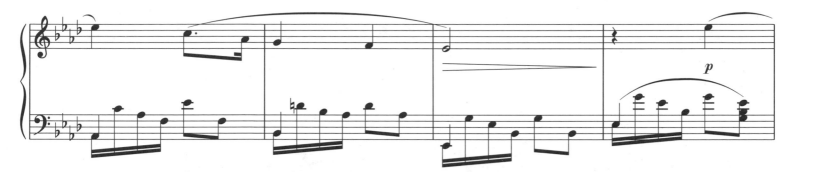

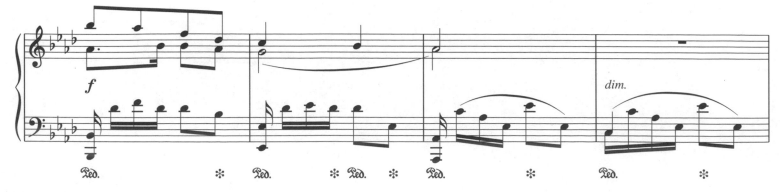

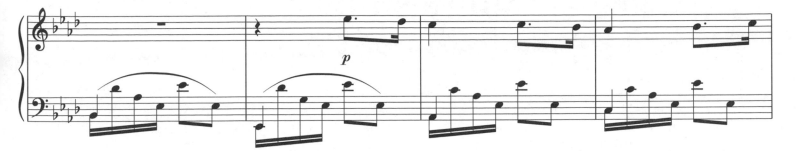

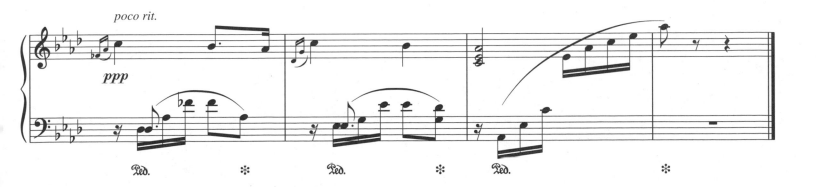

Anitra's Dance
from PEER GYNT Suite

Edvard Grieg
1843–1907
Op. 46, No. 3

Tempo di Mazurka (♩ = 160)

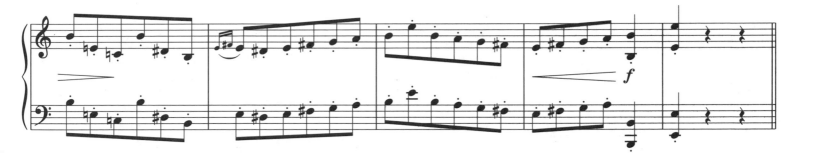

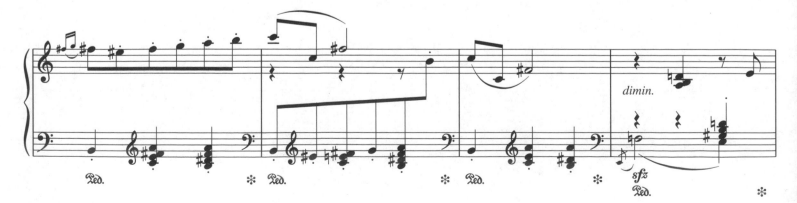

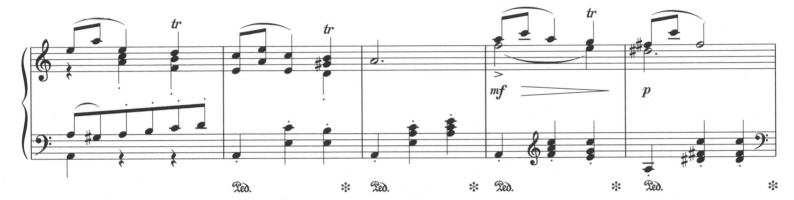

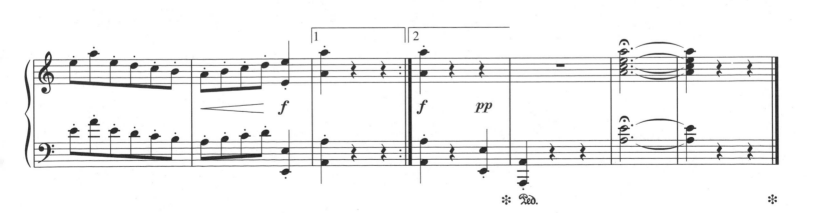

Wedding Day at Troldhaugen

from LYRIC PIECES, BOOK 8

Edvard Grieg
1843–1907
Op. 65, No. 6

Tempo di Marcia un poco vivace

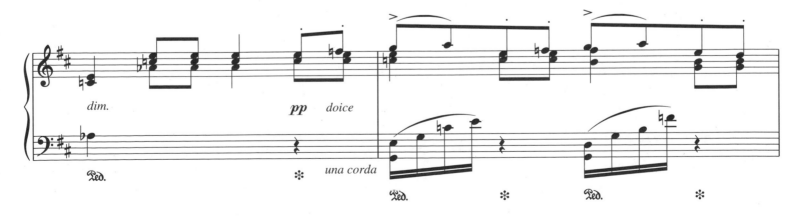

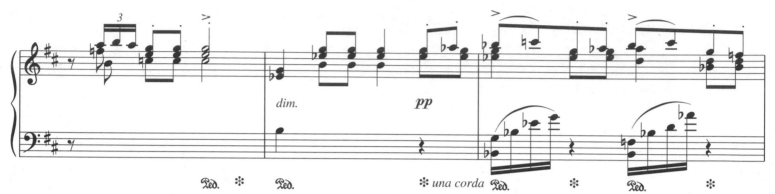

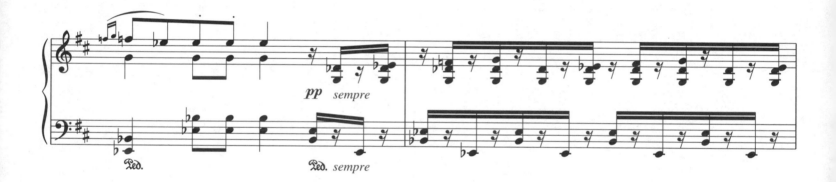

124

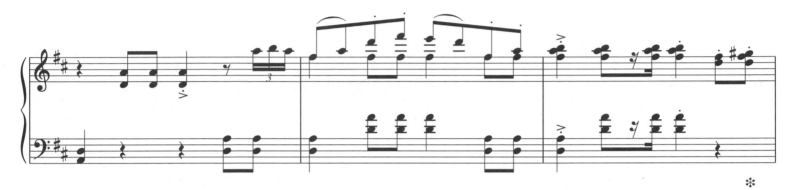

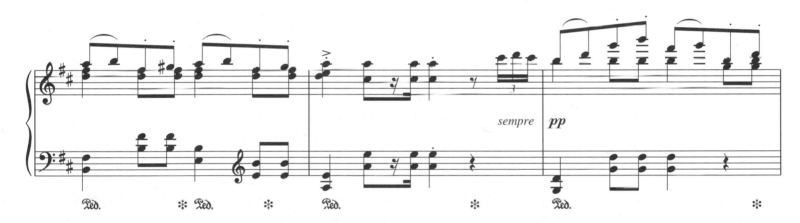

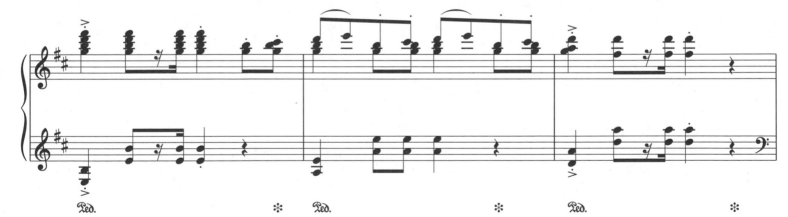

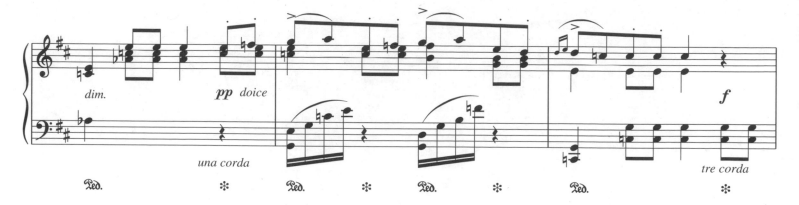

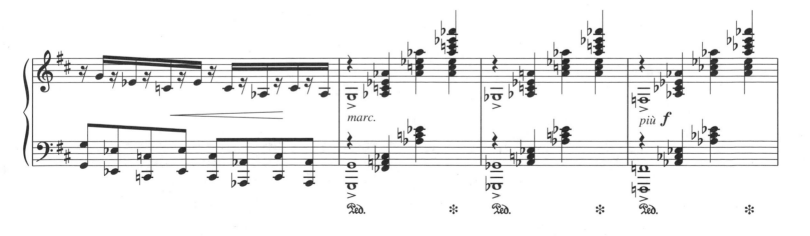

130

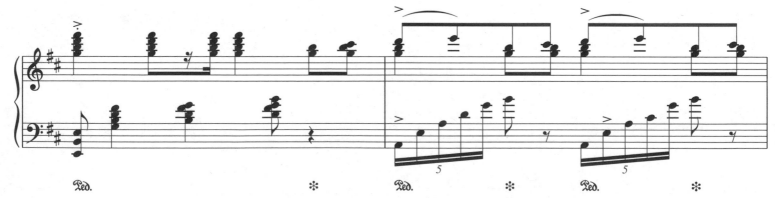

131

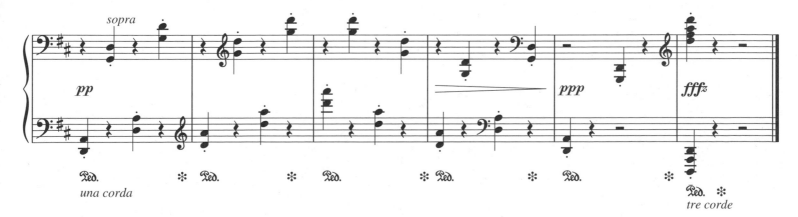

March of the Trolls
from LYRIC PIECES, BOOK 5

Edvard Grieg
1843–1907
Op. 54, No. 3

Allegretto moderato

staccato

cresc. poco a poco

tre corde

molto

ff

8va -

8va -

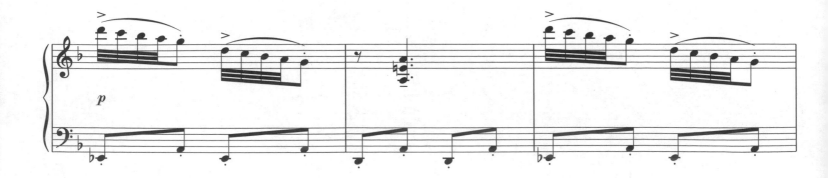

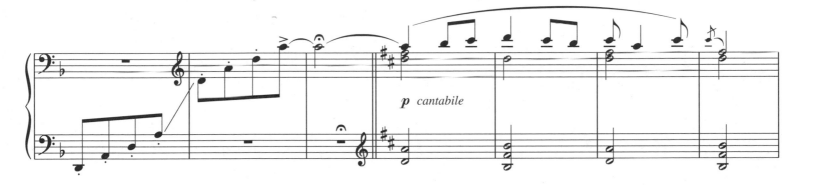

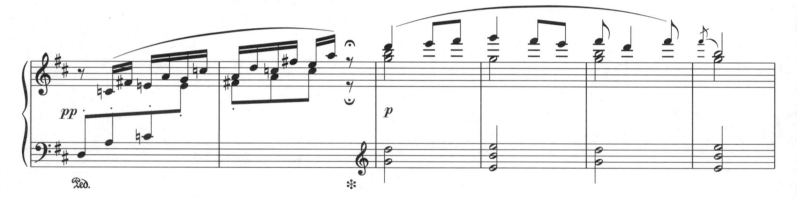

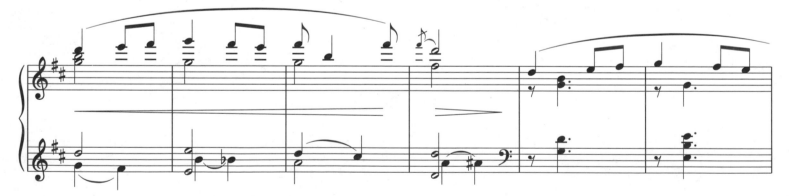

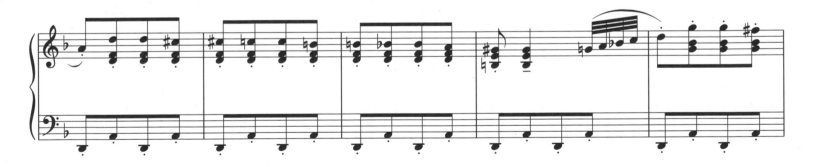

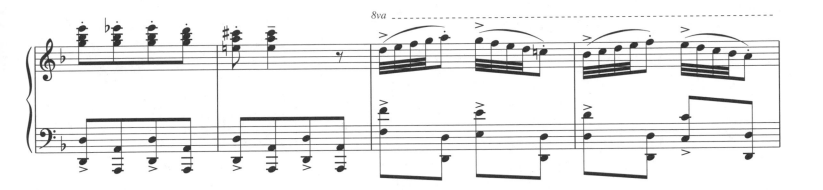

The Easy Winners

Scott Joplin
1868–1917

Introduction
Not fast

Maple Leaf Rag

Scott Joplin
1868–1917

Tempo di marcia

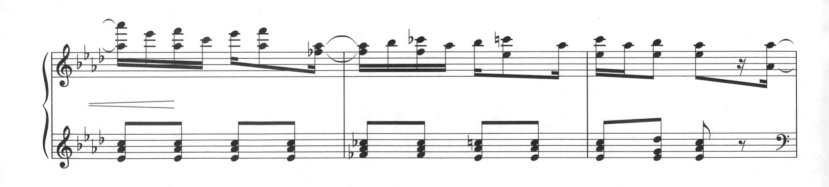

Consolation I

Franz Liszt
1811–1886

Andante con moto

dolce

Ped.   *

a tempo

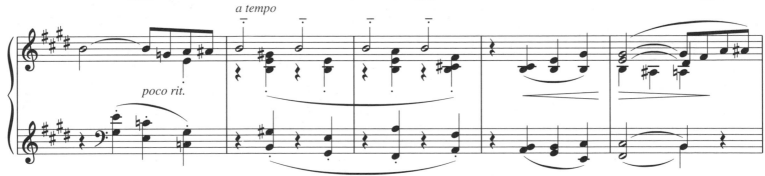

poco rit.

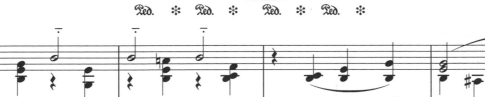

Ped.   *   Ped.   *   Ped.   *   Ped.   *

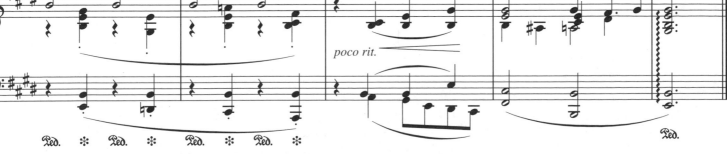

poco rit.

Ped.   *   Ped.   *   Ped.   *   Ped.   *   Ped.

Consolation II

Franz Liszt
1811–1886

Un poco più mosso

154

a tempo

ben marcato ed espressivo   il   canto

cantando

appassionato

poco rit.

accentato ed espressivo assai

smorz.

155

Consolation III

Franz Liszt
1811–1886

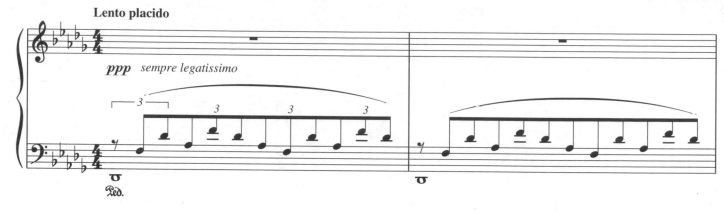

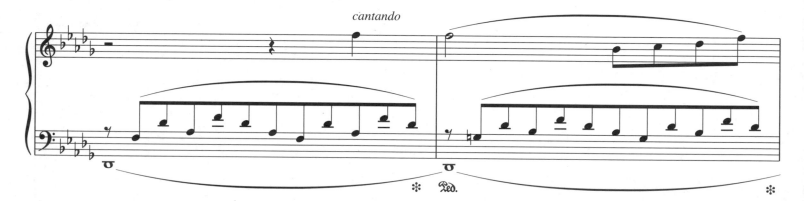

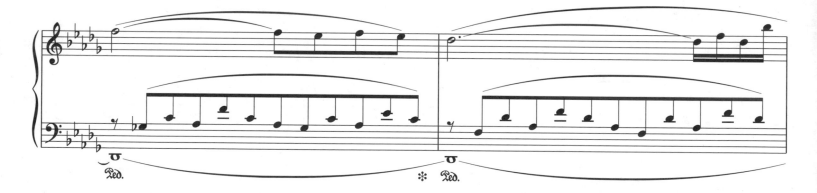

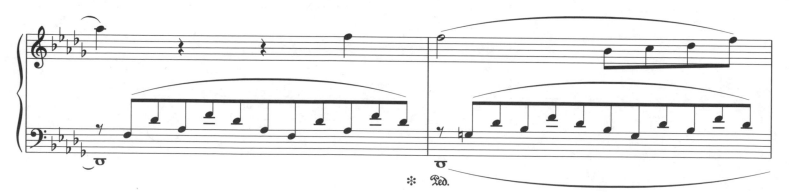

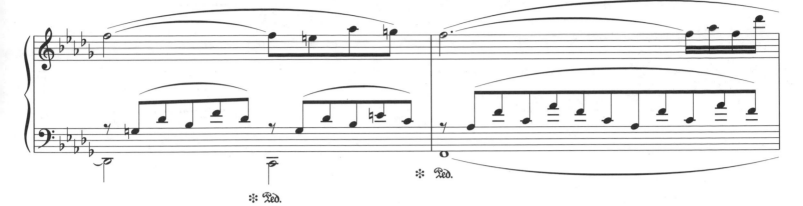

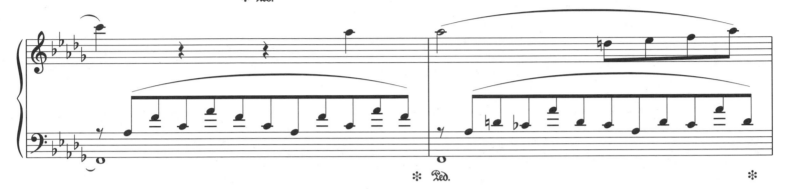

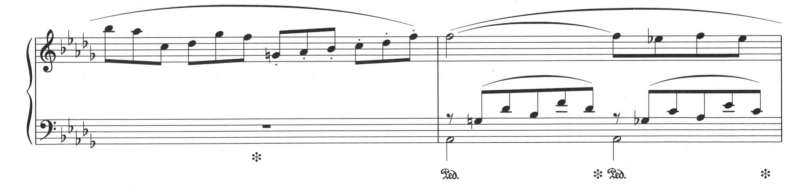

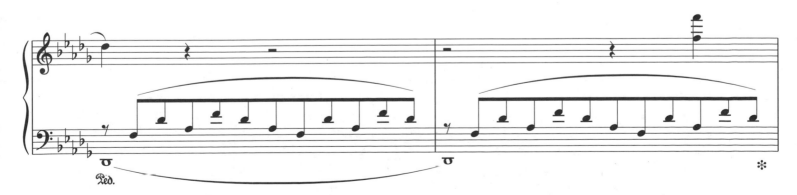

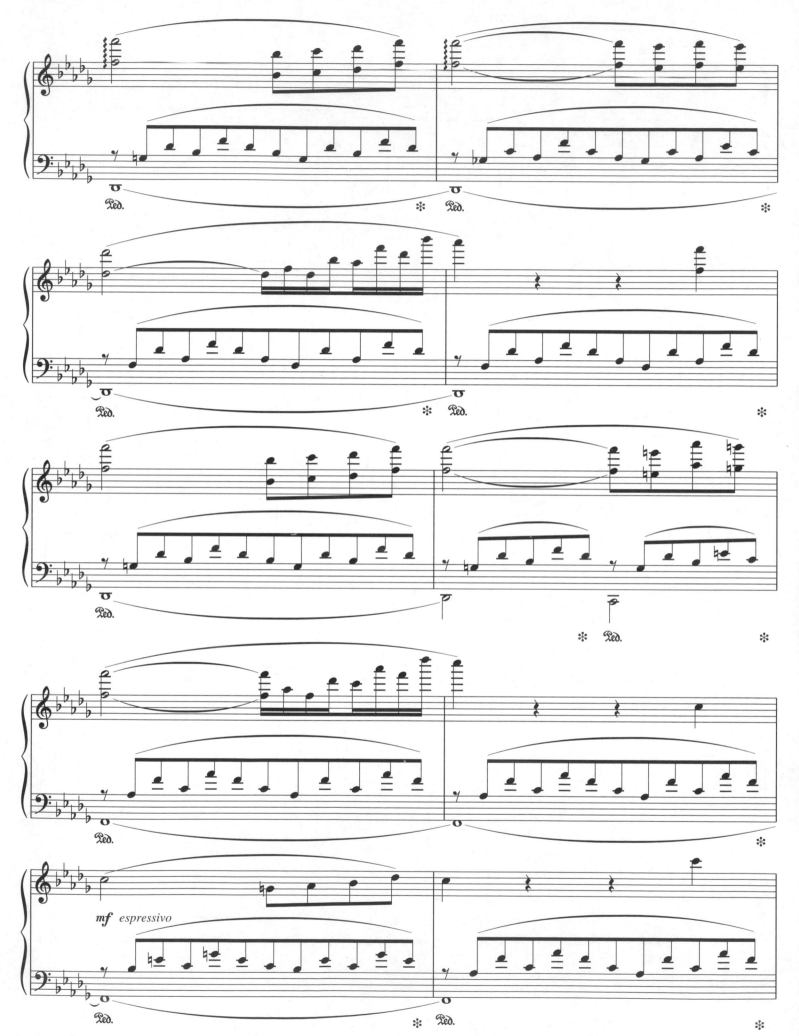

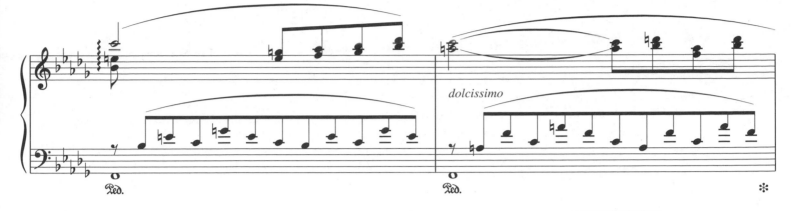

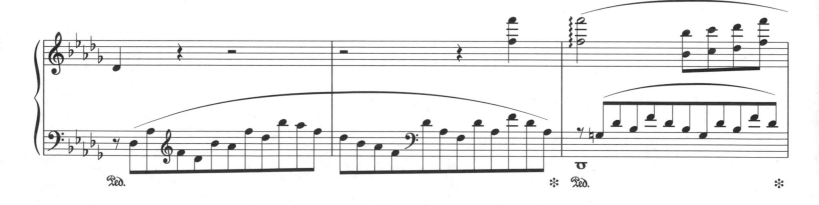

Fantasia in D Minor

Wolfgang Amadeus Mozart
1756–1791
K. 397

Andante

Presto

Tempo primo

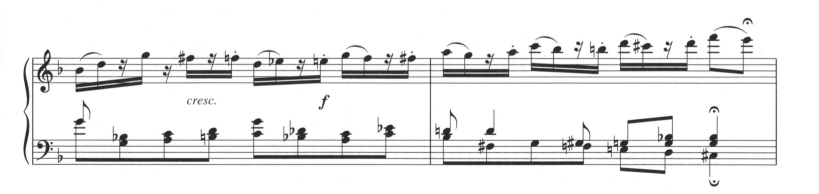

Presto

Tempo primo

Allegretto

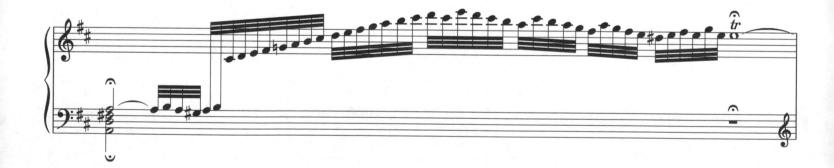

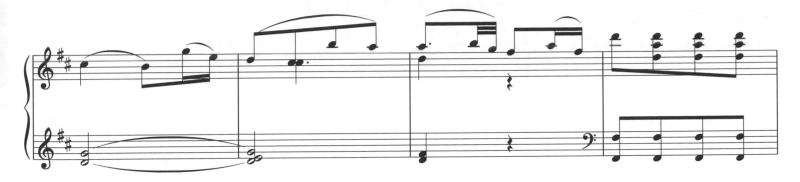

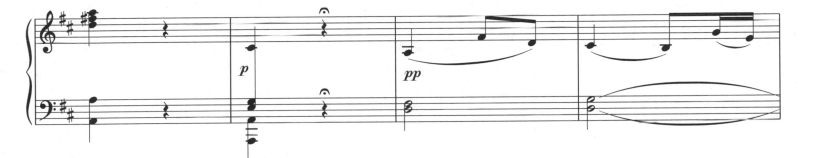

Variations on
"Ah, vous dirais-je, maman"
(Twinkle, Twinkle, Little Star)

Wolfgang Amadeus Mozart
1756–1791
K. 265

Theme
Allegretto

1st- *mf*
2nd- *pp*

Var. I

mp

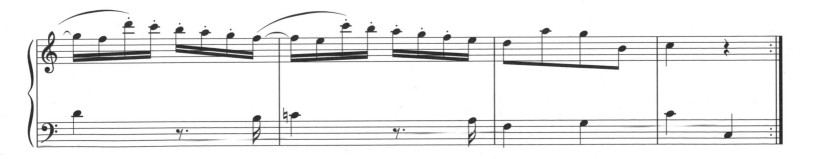

Var. II

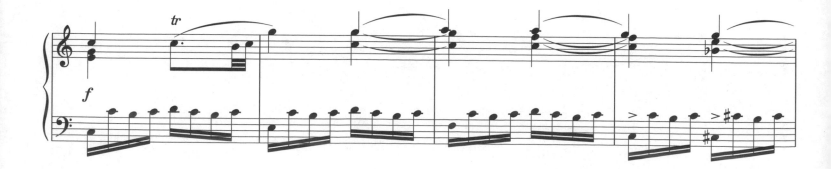

Var. III

Var. IV

f

legato

sempre *f*

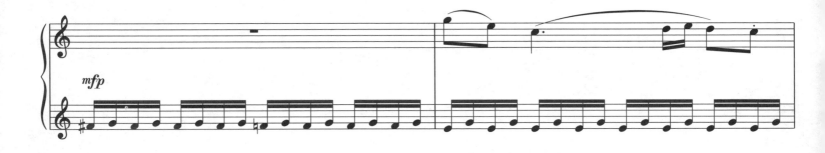

Fantasia in D Minor

Wolfgang Amadeus Mozart
1756–1791
K. 397

Andante

Presto

Tempo primo

Presto

Tempo primo

Allegretto

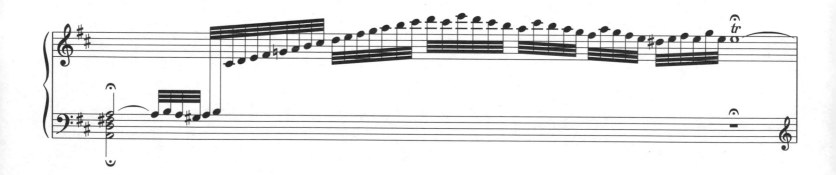

rallent.

a tempo

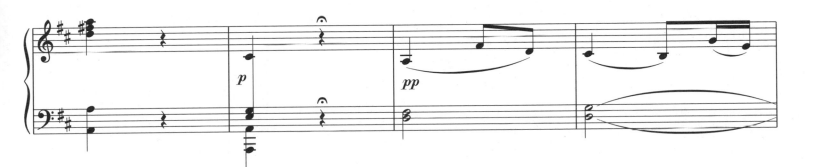

Variations on
"Ah, vous dirais-je, maman"

(Twinkle, Twinkle, Little Star)

Wolfgang Amadeus Mozart
1756–1791
K. 265

Theme
Allegretto

1st- *mf*
2nd- *pp*

Var. I

mp

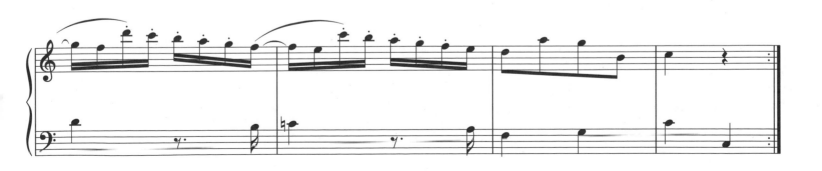

Var. II

Var. III

Var. IV

f

legato

sempre *f*

Var. V

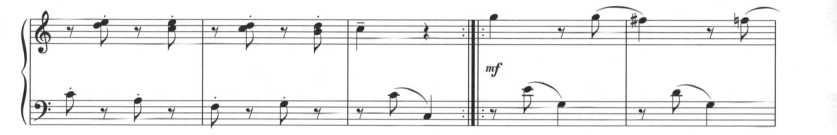

Var. VI

Var. VII

Andante
Second Movement
from SONATA in A Major

Franz Schubert
1797-1828
Op. 120 (D. 664)

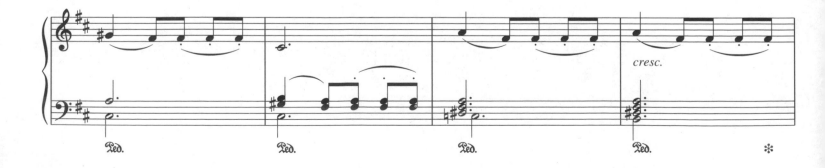

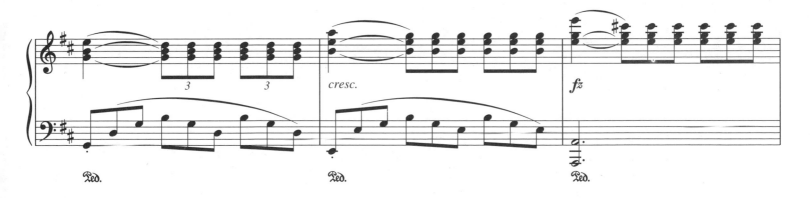

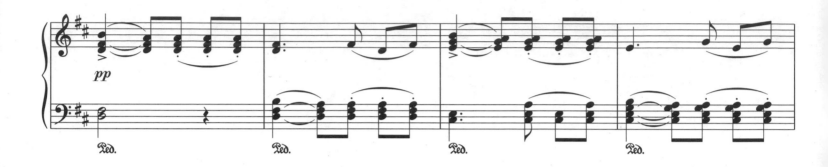

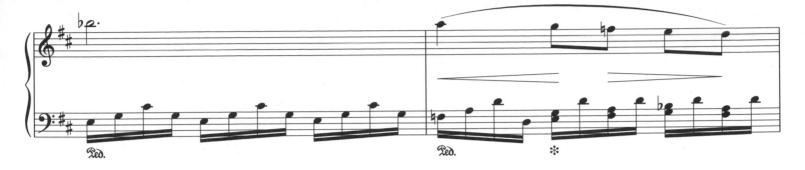

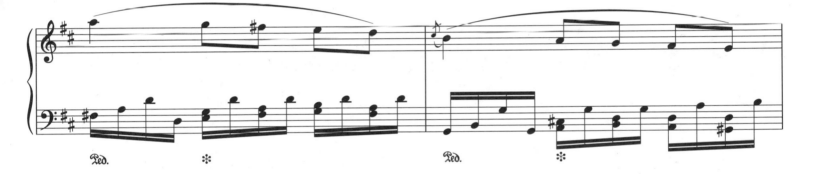

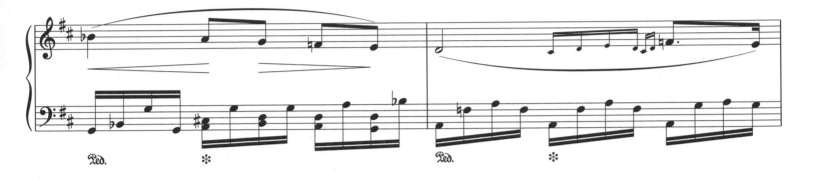

Impromptu in A-flat Major

Franz Schubert
1797-1828
Op. 142 (D. 935)

Ped.   Ped.   Ped.   *Ped. simile*

decresc.

Ped.   Ped.   Ped.

pp

Ped.   Ped.   Ped.   Ped.   Ped.   Ped.   Ped.

f

Ped.   Ped.   Ped.   Ped.   Ped.

Ped.   Ped.   Ped.   Ped.   Ped.

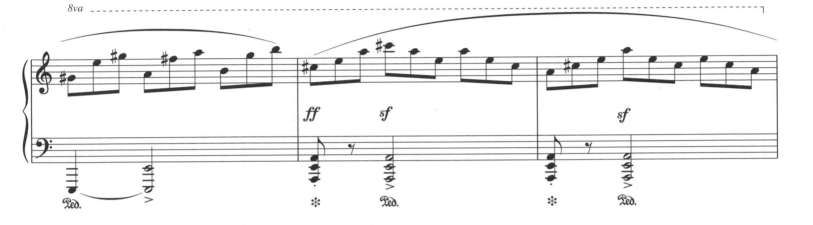

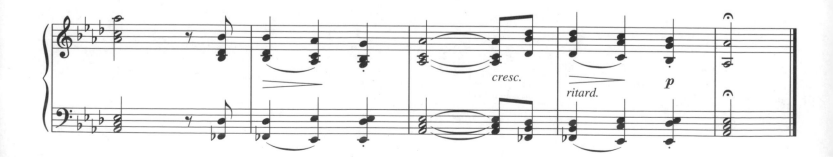

Soaring
(Aufschwung)
from PHANTASIESTÜCKE
(Fantasy Pieces)

Robert Schumann
1810-1856
Op. 12

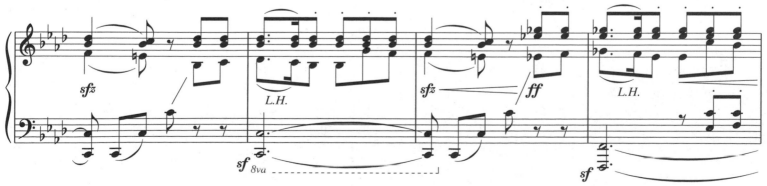

$\boldsymbol{p}$ *ma pesante*

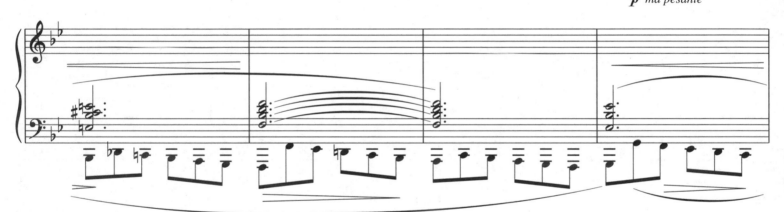

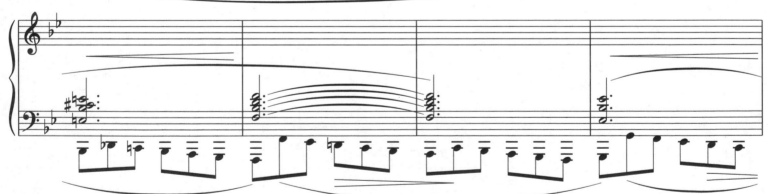

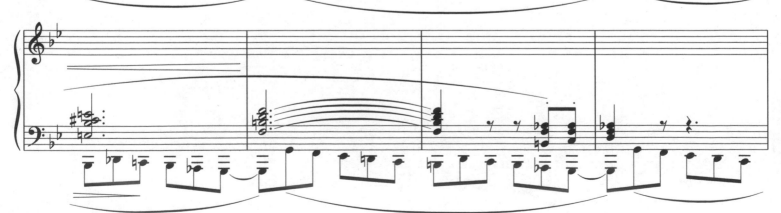

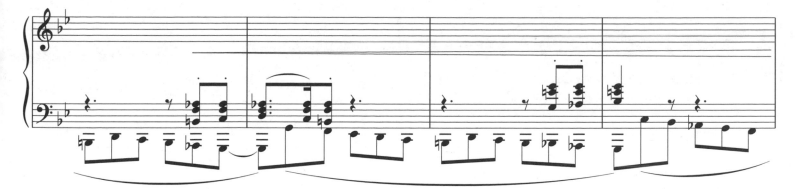

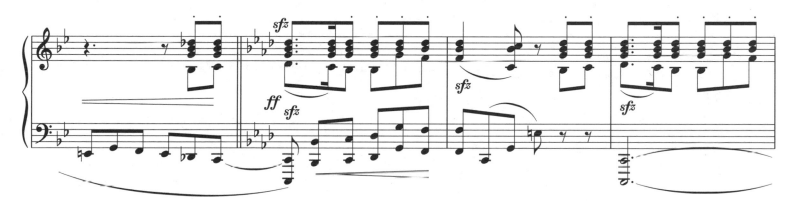

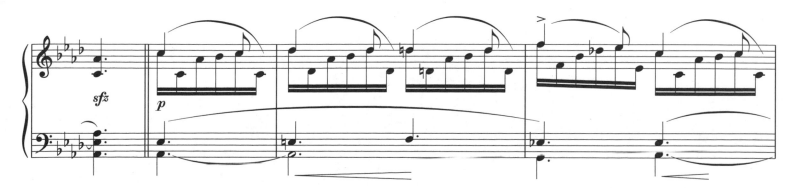

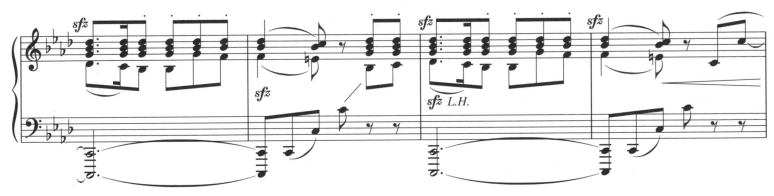

The Prophet Bird
(Vogel als Prophet)
from WALDSCENEN
(Forest Scenes)

Robert Schumann
1810-1856
Op. 82

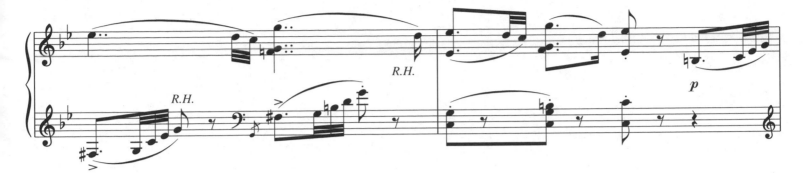

Un poco più lento

pp Verschiebung
una corda

In tempo

Prelude in C-sharp Minor

Sergei Rachmaninoff
1873-1943
Op. 3, No. 2

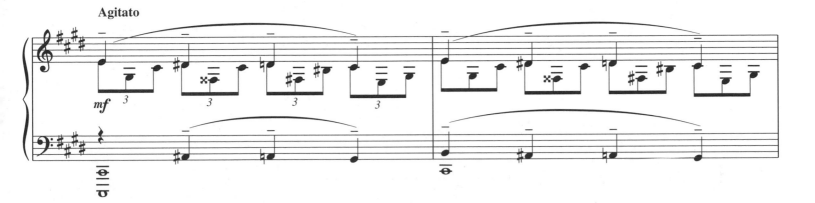

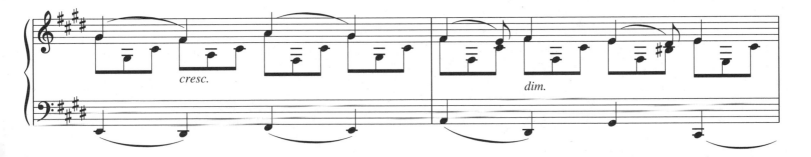

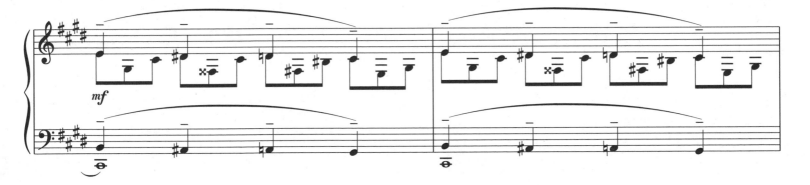

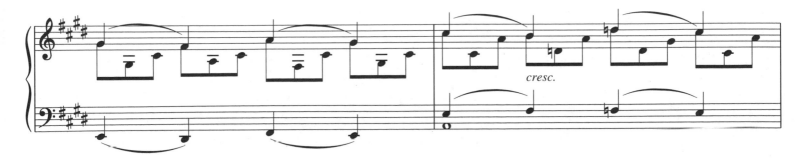

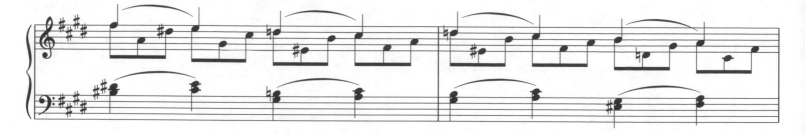

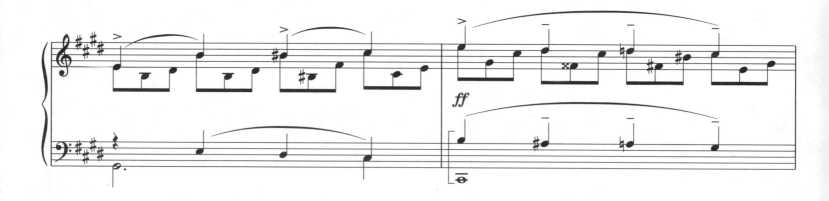

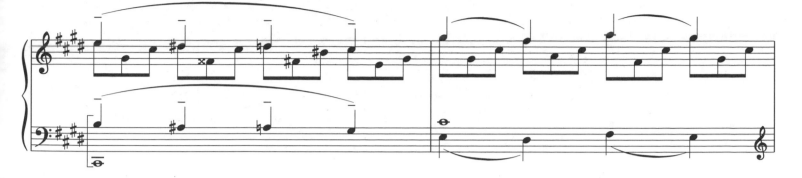

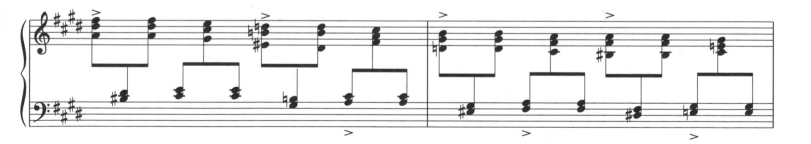

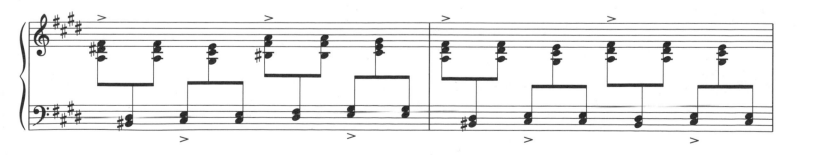

Tempo I

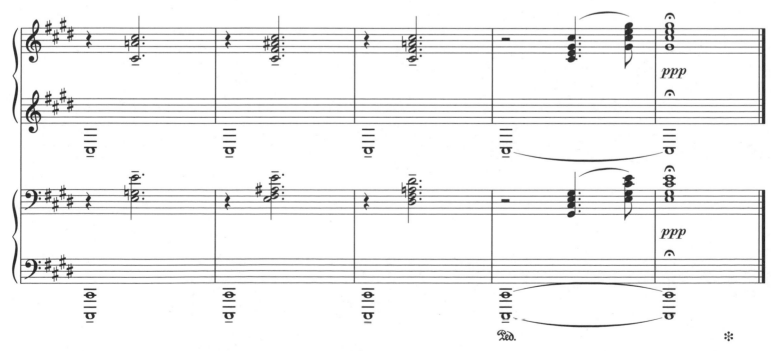

Romance

Pyotr Il'yich Tchaikovsky
1840-1893
Op. 5

poco a poco accel.

cresc.

Allegro energico

mf

f

ff

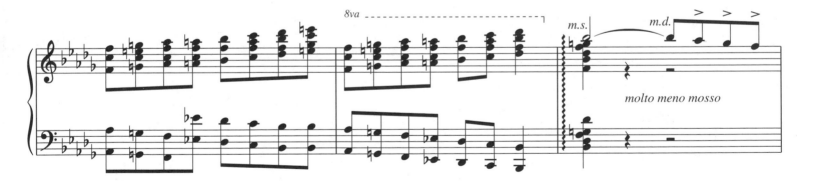

Tempo I

Chanson triste
from DOUZE MORCEAUX

Pyotr Il'yich Tchaikovsky
1840-1893
Op. 40, No. 2

Allegro non troppo
la melodia con molta espressione

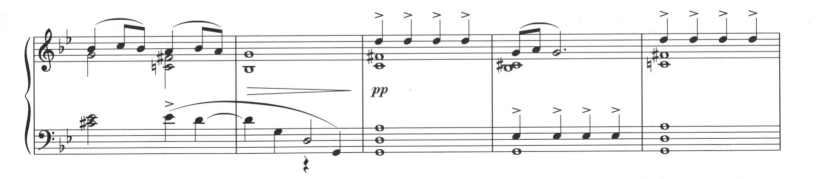

Chanson napolitaine

from ALBUM POUR ENFANTS

Pyotr Il'yich Tchaikovsky
1840-1893
Op. 39, No. 18

Moderato (♩ = 92)